HIDDEN HISTORY
of
COLUMBIA COUNTY
NEW YORK

Allison Guertin Marchese

Published by The History Press
Charleston, SC 29403
www.historypress.net

Copyright © 2014 by Allison Guertin Marchese
All rights reserved

Front cover: Delsarte class at Claverack College. *Courtesy of the Columbia County Hisotical Society, Kinderhook, New York.*
Back cover, top: Hudson street scene, late 1800s. *Courtesy of Jon and April Meredith, Kinderhook, New York.*

First published 2014

Manufactured in the United States

ISBN 978.1.62619.395.6

Library of Congress CIP data applied for.

Notice: The information in this book is true and complete to the best of our knowledge. It is offered without guarantee on the part of the author or The History Press. The author and The History Press disclaim all liability in connection with the use of this book.

All rights reserved. No part of this book may be reproduced or transmitted in any form whatsoever without prior written permission from the publisher except in the case of brief quotations embodied in critical articles and reviews.

HIDDEN HISTORY
of
COLUMBIA COUNTY
NEW YORK

I dedicate this book to Adam, my love and the man who calmly steadies my directionals in all kinds of weather.

Contents

Acknowledgements	9
Introduction	11
1: Austerlitz	15
2: Chatham	33
3: Claverack	53
4: Hudson	73
5: Kinderhook	85
6: New Lebanon	95
7: Taghkanic	109
8: Valatie	121
Bibliography	131
About the Author	143

Acknowledgements

Thank you to the following people for providing me with assistance and for sharing information and images. Many of the people managing history information in Columbia County and beyond are volunteers. They do an amazing job and donate their own personal time. I thank them especially for their help.

Karrie Allen, editor of the *Chatham Courier*
Bob Balcom, organizer of Friends Burial Ground at Rayville/Raville Quaker Cemetery
Lucy Bowen, Molly Ames, Betsy Bowen Connor and their dad, the late Croswell Bowen
Karen Carney and Moira O'Grady, volunteers at Austerlitz Historical Society at Old Austerlitz
Chatham Village Library
Claverack Library
Columbia County Historical Society
Starlyn D'Angelo, Shaker Heritage Society
Debbie Freinberg, owner of Mom and Pops Antiques, Valatie, New York
Hudson Area Library Association and the History Room attendants
Janine and Kurt Kilty, antique collectors
Rich Kraham, editor of the *Chatham Press*
Lisa LaMonica, author and history sister
Whitney Landis, editor at The History Press

Acknowledgements

Jean LaPorta, Claverack Historical Society
Jon and April Meredith, collectors, Kinderhook, New York
Dawn Olsen, Martin Van Buren National Historic Site
Holly Peppe, Millay scholar and literary executor, the Edna St. Vincent Millay Society at Steepletop
Barrie Reightler and Cindy Duebler, Maryland Horse Breeders Association
Cheryl Rogers, Taghkanic town clerk
Jacqueline Rogers, illustrator, and Jana Laiz, author
Lee Sharp and Elizabeth Powhida, volunteers at Valatie Library
Jennifer Stoner, Ghent Historical Society
Jeannine Mathieu Tonetti and Doug Banker, volunteers at the Lebanon Valley Historical Society
Linda Walsh, administrative assistant, Immaculate Conception/St. Joseph's Parish, New Lebanon, New York
Martha Wetherbee, author/collector
Gail Blass Wolczanski, Chatham Village Historical Society

I would also like to acknowledge the many people who support the preservation of history in Columbia County. Thank you.

Introduction

In 1989, I moved to Columbia County. I like to call it a time of transition. I moved here by myself during a divorce, started a new job and rented a very small apartment in the back of a historic house in Old Chatham.

To clear my head, I took long walks. I first walked on long stretches of straight, grassy paths that once served as tracks for the old railroad lines, and then I hiked up and down sparsely inhabited dirt roads and county routes that barely show up on any map. My ramblings grew in length, and sometimes, I'd be gone for two or three hours unaware that so much time had passed.

Though I had spent twelve great years in New York City working in public relations and traversing noisy concrete streets, I grew up among craggy apple orchards near silent meadows and abandoned barns in a little town in Connecticut in the 1960s and '70s. Making my way to Columbia County to collect my thoughts and start again was, in a number of ways, like coming home.

On these walking excursions, I took in the beauty of the countryside and the character of the old homes. I passed graveyards off in the distant woods and tried to make out the faded painted signs on the sides of buildings. I got to know people in town, and they told me tales of the past. The red shack by the side of the road on Route 13 with the crusty paint and sagging, moss-covered roof was once an old blacksmith shop. On Depot Lane, the old train station was still intact. The ruins by the creek bed by the bridge were once the largest paper mill in the area. A Civil War cemetery was just around the corner. I was intrigued.

Introduction

Author's house at the turn of the century. *Courtesy of Jon and April Meredith, Kinderhook, New York.*

Fast-forward five years. My life had changed, but my address was nearly the same. I purchased a historic 1740 Colonial in Malden Bridge with my significant other, Adam. It turned out to be the oldest house in the hamlet and was a mere two miles from where I started.

One day while in the living room of our beloved neighbor Bill Clerk, I leafed through a heavy, oversized book on his shelf called *The History of Columbia County*. On the first page was an inscription to his mother, Lucy Vine Clerk, who had lived in Malden Bridge in Bill's family home in the '30s. Inside the book was a detailed account of the towns within the county with beautiful illustrations, etchings, portraits and maps. Bill was a truly generous person. We lived across the creek from each other, and on one of his visits to our house, he brought me the book. Bill had a habit of doing that—giving you objects you admired from his enormous collection of wonderful things.

The history book took a place of honor on our own shelf, but there it stayed. In the years to follow, I didn't do as much walking alone, but the impulse to explore nagged me. Whenever I could, I would drive around, and once or twice, I sneaked into abandoned houses and scaled impossible back roads just to see what was there. Then, I found the dump.

Call me crazy, but because our house was an old stagecoach stop, I had a theory that the overnight guests traveling from Albany to Boston would be so afraid of losing their valuables to either Indians or thieves en route that they would bury them in our backyard and retrieve them on the return trip.

Introduction

After a big rain, I walked around our yard, which slopes down a large hill and eventually meets the rocky shore of the Kinderhook Creek. When I found my first artifact—a shard of an old pot wedged in a pile of mud and soggy, dead leaves—I couldn't wait to show it off. Since then I've turned up many interesting things: a gold compact, a perfume bottle, a silver box, a toy gun, medicine jars and an Indian fossil or two.

My digging into history didn't stay in the backyard. Fast-forward again: I revisited the book my neighbor had given me. It was written by Captain Franklin Ellis in 1878, with pages dominated by lawyers and land ownership. Informative, yes, but it didn't satisfy me. I searched for something published more recently, a book perhaps that knitted the full story of the county together. I was surprised to find there were no books written that looked more closely at the peculiar bits and fragments of history from the area. I was dying to read something that might explain quirky places and unusual facts and that recalled details about what happened daily, in real life to real people. What I did find were some local history books about Native Americans and early settlements of a few individual towns, but to be honest, they were disappointing. I started combing antique books on my own, and for amusement, I read ancient newspapers. I visited historic home sites, area museums and cemeteries. After a while, the hidden history began rising to the surface. Unearthing it completely was a notion I could not get out of my mind.

I drew up a proposal and submitted it to this publisher. I e-mailed it across the vast and largely uncharted galaxy called cyberspace. I waited. Fast-forward for the last time, to the present, and *The Hidden History of Columbia County* is complete.

Yet I can't forget that this all started with Captain Ellis. In his book on Columbia County, Ellis sets the scene. In chapter two, Ellis begins with, "The White Man's First Visit, and the Indians Whom He Found Here." Imagine the beginning the way he described it:

> *In the year 1609, and in the month of September, a small and lonely-looking vessel came in from the ocean and sailed towards the west, along the south shore of Long Island. Her people scanned the shore closely watching for inlets and harbors, until at last they came to where, behind a bare and barren point, they saw an inviting bay, which seemed to extend far away inland towards the north; and into this, after careful sounding, they entered and dropped their anchor in a sheltered roadstead, "where the water was alive with fish."*

Introduction

This is when Hudson found the Bay of New York. They traveled again in the Dutch ship the *Half Moon* with Englishman Henry Hudson as its captain, along with Robert Juet, his clerk, and a crew of twenty sailors both Dutch and English. They began their voyage out of Amsterdam, seeking passage, a northeastern or northwestern route, to China and the Indies.

Hudson and his crew next discovered an estuary, which from outward appearances, looked like it could be the path he sought. It turned out to be what we know as Staten Island. He moved upriver, past West Point, and then near the Catskills, he anchored. This is the moment he met the Mohicans. At a geographical point of latitude 42°18" N, which most believe and Ellis states "was in the present town of Stockport," was when the commander of the *Half Moon*, Henry Hudson, became the first white man who ever set foot within the unspoiled countryside that is now Columbia County.

I want to say that I am both grateful and excited to have had the opportunity to write this book and tell you about the extraordinarily beautiful place that I love and call home.

I used to have a friend, Margaret, from Lithuania, who was forever mixing up common clichés. For example, rather than using the expression, "Nice house, nobody home," she would say, "Nice house, no curtains." In the spirit of my friend, let me say that this book is just "the tip of the ice cube."

In that what you will read is limited to about thirty-five thousand words, I unfortunately left out many, many fascinating pieces of the Columbia County story. I was, however, able to illuminate the true texture and diversity of the area by describing people and places in eight of Columbia County's eighteen towns.

Oh, and one more thing: This book is by no rational stretch of the imagination intended to be the final word on how Columbia County was discovered, developed, founded or formed. I humbly hand over that task to scholars and historians who may, someday, write another book. *The Hidden History of Columbia County* is an exploration, a walk through time, if you will, meant to be enjoyed. And if bringing this book to you helps to preserve this incredible place, then I will have accomplished what I set out to do.

I
AUSTERLITZ

ALL THE WAY UP TO AUSTERLITZ

As the story goes, Austerlitz, New York, started as an unruly area with rugged hillsides and tangled forests covering six square miles. It was first settled in 1750 by squatters from Connecticut in the east and land grants from the State of Massachusetts. The first settler, Judah Monis Lawrence, along with the twelve Spencer families, the Powells, the Richmonds and the Pratts, divided the land into lots in 1757 and laid out logical highways. Within the land grants was a minor tract of land along the Green River belonging to the Mohicans, which the townspeople negotiated for purchase.

After some intense infighting about who owned which land titles, the issue was finally put to rest after an unsuccessful visit to the mother country, and in 1791, a decision was made to break off pieces of neighboring towns, including Chatham, Canaan and Hillsdale, and mold them together into a new town. When it came time to name the town around 1818, the Spencer families who first settled it took charge and named it Spencertown. But thanks to Martin Van Buren, the New York State senator at the time (whose name pops up quite often in the history of Columbia County), the town was named Austerlitz. It seems that originally there was a push to call the town New Ulm, but Martin Van Buren was a big fan of Napoleon and had been more than a bit annoyed that one of his political opponents had won a fight to name another local town Waterloo. It is reported that Van

Hidden History of Columbia County, New York

A Columbia County country road, postcard. *Collection of Jon and April Meredith, Kinderhook, New York.*

Buren vehemently insisted that the town be called Austerlitz (referencing the famous battle). MVB won the argument, and the name stuck.

For the most part, Austerlitz is still as untouched and natural as it was when it was merely rural dirt roads that wound around sloping hills, with still only about 1,600 people currently making up the town and little commercial development ever really getting a foothold. Early on, the town adopted a plan to favor "the poor man by allowing his animals to graze in the highway." Its most notable places include Beebe Hill and Harvey Mountain State Forests, which cover about three thousand acres of preserved town land with Harvey Mountain being the highest elevation in Columbia County at 2,065 feet.

Near the summit of Harvey Mountain, a wild blueberry field exists that historically provided revenue for residents and attracted many to the area. To this day, blueberries in Austerlitz are a big deal, prompting an annual festival that gathers thousands of berry enthusiasts.

Though it is a relatively small place, a fair amount of history took place amid its hills and valleys. Perhaps due to its elevation and remote location, Austerlitz is most definitely still a bit unsettled. In fact, the local townspeople seem to think that it's in its own unique climate zone. In truth, Austerlitz is part of the Taconic Mountain Range and creates the eastern border

The Harvey Hotel in Austerlitz in the mid-nineteenth century. *Collection of Jon and April Meredith, Kinderhook, New York.*

between Columbia County and the Berkshires of Massachusetts. There are a few notable facts about the town, including its being credited with the invention of the first grass mower.

DOWN HILL RACER

Back in the late 1940s, Austerlitz was surprisingly a favorite place for skiers. The slope was a primitive operation, utilizing thick, course tow ropes measuring up to 750 feet long to haul adventurous skiers up the mostly forested hill. The ski area was created by Howard Hirsch of New York City and named Mountain Ten because it was constructed in part by veterans of the WWII Tenth Mountain Division, a highly specialized team of soldiers trained in winter warfare. The ski area boasted the longest tow rope in North America, and locals said you had to have "a strong grip" to make it to the top. Though the original lodge was destroyed by fire, serious hikers can still find the remains of the old lodge's fireplace deep in the woods. Up at the top of the old ski trail is the motor "shack" that operated the ropes.

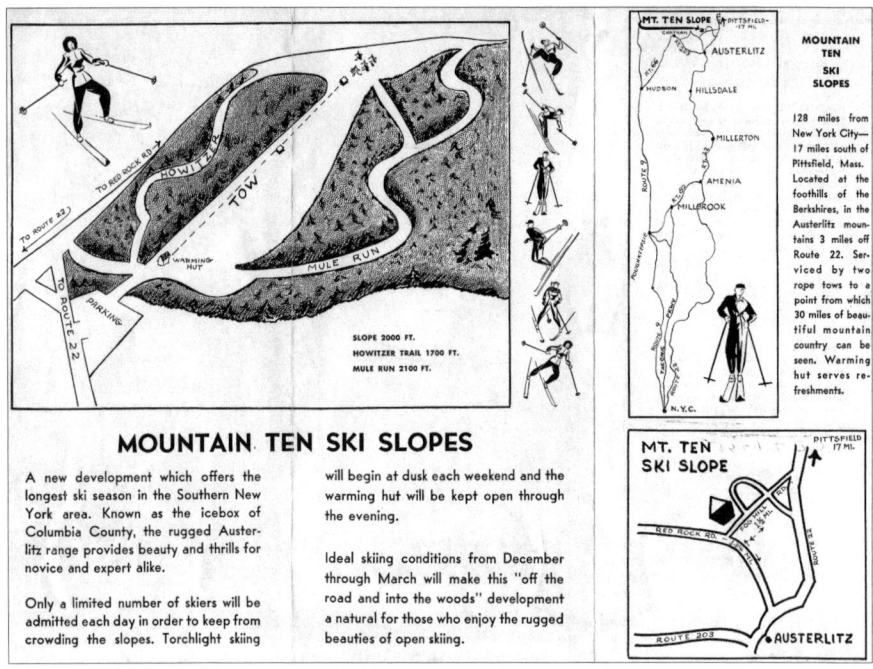

Mountain Ten Ski Slopes brochure. *Courtesy of the Austerlitz Historical Society, Austerlitz, New York.*

Yet amid this remarkably peaceful backdrop, one of the most gruesome murders occurred in the 1880s, attracting national and international attention and raising the question of whether or not gold was hidden in the Austerlitz hills.

Hanging Around

It was certainly not every day that an eighty-year-old man was hanged in Columbia County for crimes so abhorrent as this, yet desperate men do desperate things.

Oscar Fritz Allan Beckwith was born in Austerlitz in 1810. His father was Joshua and his mother was Mercy Calkins, a descendant of Miles Standish. He had a younger sister by the name of Phebe, or Phoebe, born in 1820.

His victim was Simon Adolphus Vandercook, who was the eighth of eleven children born to Simon S. and Elizabeth Snyder Vandercook of Rensselaer County, New York.

AUSTERLITZ

According to accounts, Vandercook was a schemer and was part of the infamous Rensselaer County Gold and Silver Mining Scandal of 1867. Beckwith came with his own unseemly baggage. He carried with him a lengthy list of accusations, including assault, larceny and counterfeiting. Both men had failed marriages. Beckwith had left his wife in Egremont, Massachusetts.

When Vandercook and Beckwith finally met in 1878, Beckwith owned land in Austerlitz that he bought seeking his fortune in gold. Beckwith, Vandercook and another man agreed to divide the profits of mining the land into thirds. Greed seemed to be driving the partnership, so Vandercook moved close by to neighboring Alford, Massachusetts, to begin working the mine. When nothing of value was uncovered, Vandercook grew impatient and started furiously logging the land and selling off the trees for firewood.

Beckwith was incensed at discovering Vandercook's sudden wealth and could assume only that he had been robbed of his fair share of the mine profits. This misunderstanding put into motion a chain of grisly events. On a frigid January day in 1882, the men fought in the shack that Beckwith had constructed for himself on the side of Harvey Mountain in Austerlitz, and with an axe, Beckwith delivered a fatal blow. The axe played an even greater role in the crime in that Beckwith then dismantled the body of Simon Vandercook, hewing him into bits and parts quite unrecognizable as what was once a human form.

To eat one's prey holds a tremendous amount of significance in this story. As a sign of victory, dominance or sheer insanity, Beckwith carved his partner into a culinary delicacy and feasted on him. When unusual aromas wafted from Beckwith's cabin, neighbors became suspicious, especially those who noticed Vandercook's disappearance. A party of men quickly investigated the scene in the deep woods of Austerlitz, but all that remained was bones and a thick stew.

Yet Beckwith averted immediate capture and fled, first to the caves beyond Fog Hill Road near No Bottom Pond and then on foot to Canada. The case of the Austerlitz cannibal traces a zigzagged path of near misses with the final ending occurring in Toronto. Charged with murder, Oscar Beckwith was arrested in the Parry Sound district, east of Georgian Bay, Ontario, in 1885. Reports say he was taken prisoner in a remote wilderness nearly one hundred miles from any person, place or modern convenience. His crime was characterized as being guilty of burning his victim with some portion of the body being pickled to be used as nourishment while on foot during his escape. The lawman behind the pursuit of Beckwith was Detective J.P. Gildersleeve of Kinderhook, Columbia County, New York, who said he first drafted the escapee all the way west to the Canadian Pacific coast and then turned eastward. He gathered help from Canadian wood rangers and succeeded in arresting the murderer.

The seventy-eight-year-old Beckwith was soon sentenced to hang. Just days before he was hanged, Beckwith was visited by a young reporter by the name of David C. Neefus from the *Hudson Republican*. He was the only Columbia County resident to receive an invitation to the hanging. There was great excitement in the county on March 2, 1888, from those who held a seat to watch Beckwith swing from the neck in front of the Hudson courthouse, where the gallows was erected. Before the event, Neefus visited Beckwith in his cell and later described him as "a powerfully built man, though in his late 70s, with a jutting jaw, leonine head and small beady eyes." Guarded and chained, Beckwith still managed to boast about his exploits and would sometimes become violent or go on hunger strikes. As tension increased, Beckwith was further restrained with shackles on his hands and feet. The gallows was imported from New York by a gentleman named J.B. Atkinson of Brooklyn, who was directing the hanging. He was accompanied by an unidentified gentleman responsible for tripping the mechanism that would send Beckwith to his death.

The crowds gathered early at the site of the hanging, just south of the courthouse, and women reportedly rushed the line of soldiers guarding the event, claiming they had purchased "reserved seats" at fifty cents each. Beckwith consumed a last meal of steak and toast and, dressed in a Prince Albert coat and tie, proceeded into the crowd. Just prior to the hanging, reporters were granted time to speak to the condemned man, at which time he read them a letter he had written to his daughter in which he requested that his body be buried in Austerlitz beside his father and mother

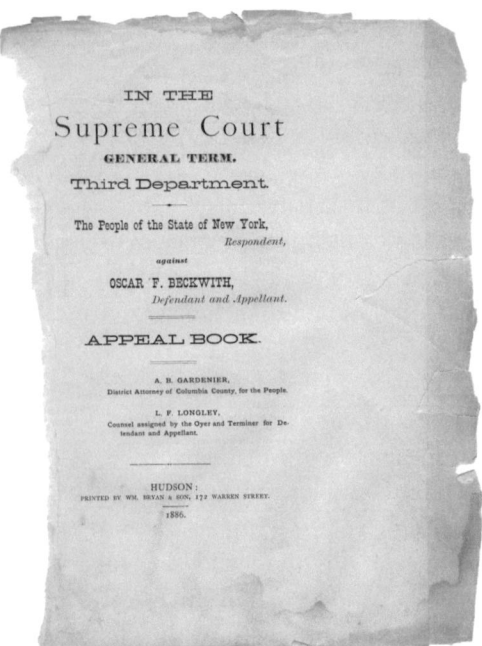

Oscar Beckwith trial papers. *Courtesy of the Austerlitz Historical Society, Austerlitz, New York.*

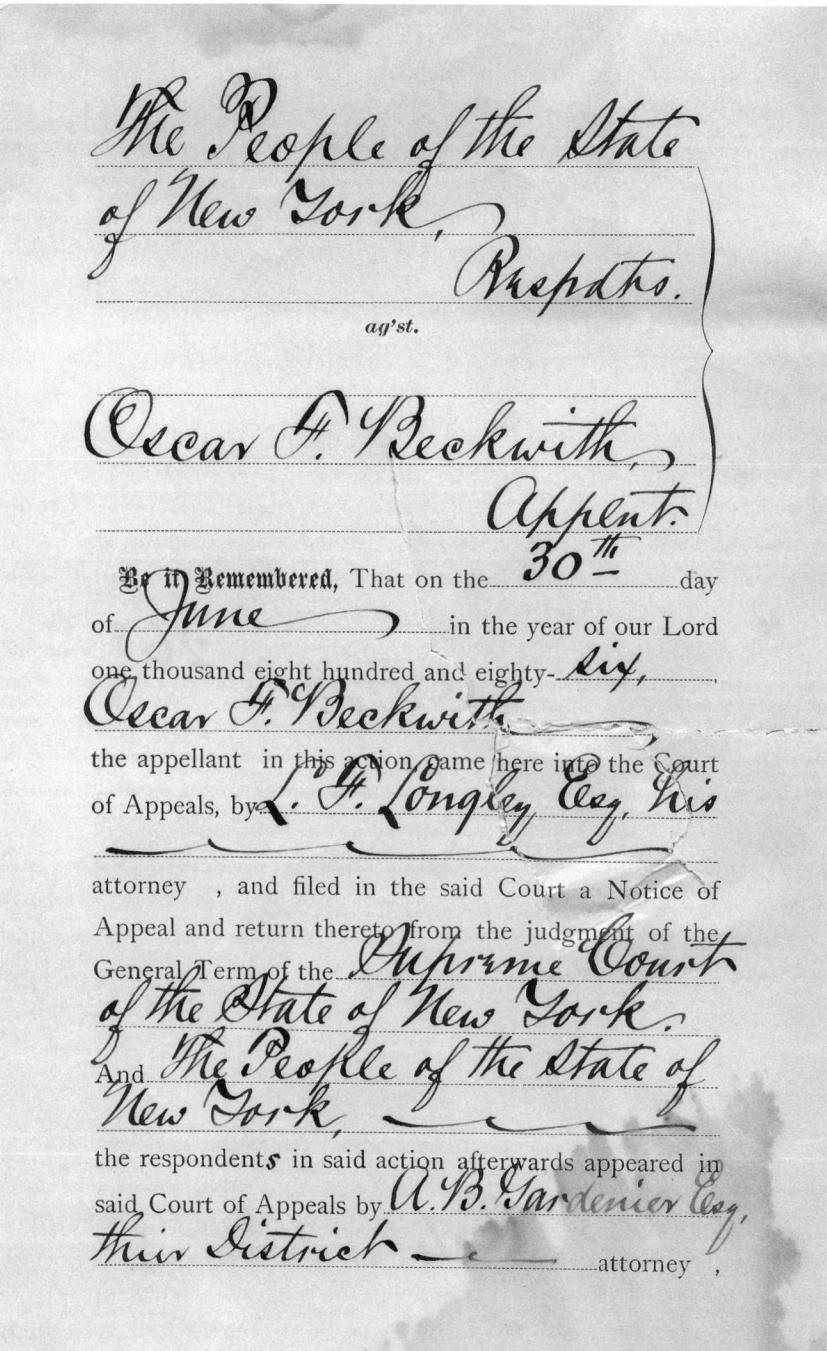

Oscar Beckwith trial papers of the Supreme Court. *Courtesy of the Austerlitz Historical Society, Austerlitz, New York.*

in the new burying ground near Kenne's. He then bid his daughter a "long farewell" and signed it: "Your loving Father Oscar Beckwith."

He said to the reporters, "Boys, goodbye, I have no confession. I have not known one person hanged in this county in the last 75 years who was guilty. They were all hanged by public opinion. I die innocent. Vandercook was killed, but not murdered." Beckwith reportedly turned ashen gray and quaked at the site of the instrument of death. Ironically, it was the sharp blow of an axe that cut a six-hundred-pound weight loose, which jerked Beckwith's body four feet in the air. It took a full fourteen minutes for Beckwith to die of a broken neck, with physicians on the scene monitoring his heart rate. When cut loose, the crowd dove for the remains of the rope that took Beckwith's life. He was the fifth person to be executed in the county, and his death on the gallows was the last on Columbia County soil.

Some years later, in 1958, a surprising discovery was made by Joseph Elliot, postmaster in nearby North Egremont, Massachusetts, who investigated the site where the murder took place in hopes of finding the gold that neither Beckwith nor his partner uncovered. Because the previous pathways up to the steep mountain site had been overgrown by pines and bushes, Elliott took a path through Varney Mountain in neighboring Massachusetts. Elliott brought along Arthur Drumm, who had reportedly visited the Beckwith cabin as a boy. They successfully dug up a number of human bones, which they brought to a local physician for verification. The doctor could say for certain that the bones were consistent with someone who had suffered the blows of a sharp object, but he couldn't say for sure whether these were the remains of Vandercook, Beckwith's victim. The question remains whether Beckwith had committed one murder or many; no one knows just how many bodies are buried on the mountain in Austerlitz.

Down, Down, Don't Drown

In the black woods of Austerlitz, a strange mist could often be seen near a road not far from the area where Beckwith mined unsuccessfully for gold. Fog Hill Road rests alongside No Bottom Pond. Some say that during his run from the law, Beckwith first escaped to the pond, which is peppered with deep holes and foreboding caves. In winter, the water is frigid, velvety blue and, as the legend goes, deep enough that if one were to throw a stone into the center, the sound of it hitting the bottom would never be heard.

AUSTERLITZ

No Bottom Pond, Austerlitz, New York. *Courtesy of the* Chatham Press, *Chatham, New York.*

Yet in summer the pond drains to a bone-dry surface with the waters disappearing into the earth through a hole in the rock and reappearing somewhere near the Green River. Local residents on Fog Hill Road near the pond have reported stories of men vanishing into the abyss and venturing into the caves where bears and large wild black cats make their homes. In the late 1950s, a local team of spelunkers made a fervent attempt at finding the "black beast of the Berkshires."

Hidden History of Columbia County, New York

The catamount was tracked to the mouth of the cave again in the 1960s by a man named "Pop" Sweet, a local Austerlitz musician. In the 1970s, Stanley E. Moore of Pittsfield, Massachusetts led a team of eleven cave explorers to the site. Much to their surprise, as they lowered themselves seven hundred feet below the floor of No Bottom Pond, they found themselves in a two-hundred-foot-deep cavern, revealing an underground arch in the first room. The second room measured about twenty by thirty feet, and a third room was well over six feet deep. In the treasure-trove of items, the spelunkers uncovered many large animal bones and antique shovels and hoes, which some surmised were once used by early miners looking for gold near the stream that runs out the back of the cave.

Poets in Nature

According to an 1873 map of area tributaries made by a gentleman known as Welcome Gott, the Green River originates at No Bottom Pond and a second tributary to the Green River is called the East Hill Stream.

For such a small rivulet, the Green River is world renowned, for it was this corner of Columbia County, on the edge of Austerlitz leading southward toward Hillsdale, that drew poets who were loved by millions. In the early 1800s, William Cullen Bryant was a young man, a Romantic and a lover of nature living near Great Barrington, Massachusetts. On

Blue Top Service Station, Green River, Austerlitz, New York. *Courtesy of Jon and April Meredith, Kinderhook, New York.*

William Cullen Bryant. *Courtesy of Library of Congress.*

one of his walks through the woods and forests, he found the Green River. Inspired to capture the essence of its beauty, Bryant penned the poem "The Green River," in which he lovingly caressed the quiet waterway with his words.

The spectacular vistas, soft streams and deep, hidden woods attracted another great poet to Austerlitz. In 1925, Edna St. Vincent Millay and her husband, Eugen Boissevain, purchased what was once the T. and W. Gooding and Ambrose Cooke home, later known as the Bailey Place, in Austerlitz, New York.

Her name has appeared in millions of documents and articles around the world, and nearly every adjective has been used to describe Edna St. Vincent Millay's unique physical appearance and the allure of her mysterious character. She generally created a new level of fame for poets and writers. Though her life began with a modest upbringing in Rockland, Maine, Millay's life tracked steadily upward on a path through Vassar College in Poughkeepsie; New York City's Greenwich Village; Paris, France; and eventually the unlikely place of Austerlitz, New York.

Her combined brilliance, dedication and determination made her one of the most talked-about people of her time. And unlike other women living in the '20s, her boundaries and notoriety were limitless. She was spirited, outspoken and became well known for a number of unusual occurrences and accomplishments. Edna St. Vincent Millay is deeply embedded in Austerlitz's hidden history.

Unknown to most, Millay has been credited with spotting a German ship off Tortola in 1940, which made the papers in Chatham, New York. She was also arrested in Boston for protesting the trial of Saecco and Vanzetti

Eugen Boissevain (left) husband of Poet, Edna St. Vincent Millay (right), taken at Millay's country estate, Steepletop, in Austerlitz. *Courtesy of the Literary Executor/Edna St. Vincent Millay Society at Steepletop, Austerlitz, New York.*

in August 1927. In 1923, Millay was the first woman and second person to win the newly minted Pulitzer Prize for Poetry. (Three people, two of them women, received Special Pulitzers for poetry prior to the award's official commencement and are now included among the poetry prize's winners.) Among other great accomplishments, Millay was credited by the *New York Times* with having written the greatest American opera, *The King's Henchman*, which was performed at the Metropolitan in New York.

Millay operated on keen intuition and sharp instincts. Yet her arrival in Austerlitz seemed almost predestined. While celebrating with friends at a party in 1923, the same year that she was awarded the Pulitzer Prize, Millay teamed up with Eugen Boissevain in a romantic game of charades. She had met the Dutch importer once before, in 1918, at the funeral of his wife, Inez Millholland, who led the way during the women's suffrage movement. Boissevain and Millay's love immediately blossomed, as they shared many interests and a passion for nature. Millay was already famous when she married Boissevain. She had published extensively, graduated from Vassar, acted in New York and written an opera. She had lived in Paris, written for *Vanity Fair* and won the Pulitzer. She was a successful poet, playwright and feminist. And perhaps because of her rapid rise to fame, her health had suffered and she was ready for a rest.

AUSTERLITZ

The couple wed quickly and toured extensively on their honeymoon. They collected a vast array of precious objects, art and memorabilia. The newlyweds took their newfound love to a remote corner of New York State, where they purchased a farm from the Baileys, along with a vast amount of land atop Harvey Mountain for just $9,000.

Millay grew up with wood-burning fires, oil lamps and water for washing heated on the stove. She lived in Maine by the seashore near windswept beaches and sweet-smelling pines. While traveling and writing, she longed for the peacefulness of her rural childhood, and for the most part, the Austerlitz farm she purchased with her new husband, Eugen Boissevain, one Sunday afternoon while on an excursion from New York City was rustic by design.

Millay's farm, like much of Austerlitz, offered field after field of low-bush blueberries, a crop that had once sustained the early settlers in the area. In all, the hilltop farm possessed seven hundred acres bursting with wildlife, freshwater springs, wild honeysuckle, purple barberry and red oak. Among the native plants and heritage apple trees was a delicate pink flowering steeplebush, a shrub that grew quietly among the undulating hills hugging the edges of the hardwood forests and cascading meadows and occasionally appearing close to the 1878 farmhouse on their property. They named their new home Steepletop in honor of the fragile shrub and soon transformed the property into a private retreat that mirrored themselves.

Herbs were planted in a neat kitchen garden, and vegetables were bedded too. Thick concrete was poured into earth trenches for a beloved spring-fed swimming pool. A barn was erected, and a masterful garden was engineered, featuring individual outdoor spaces with distinct personalities and treasures.

For Millay, Steepletop would remain her solace, her private retreat where she could live a life of a true naturalist unencumbered by the world of celebrity she had known for so many years.

She referred to Austerlitz as "wild country," and to this day that is more or less the truth. The road leading to the original seven-hundred-acre blueberry farm was nearly impassable in winter and only a well-equipped sleigh could bring the couple down the hill for the nearly five months of winter that lingered in the little town. Yet Millay would frequent the nearest town of Chatham eight miles away. Her protective husband, Boissevain, feared the open and unguarded railroad crossing that dominated Chatham Village's business district. More than once, it was reported that the couple was stranded between the widespread crossing, and they often suggested that the town install warning signals. Yet the privacy of her home in Austerlitz in the serene quiet of the natural environment was comforting and inspiring.

Edna St. Vincent Millay, 1928. *Courtesy of Edna St. Vincent Millay Society at Steepletop, Austerlitz, New York.*

She wrote frequently of the beauty of harvest on the hill, of the autumn colors, of flourishing fields atop the mountain and even of her pair of black plow horses, Molly and Tom.

Some say that Millay was the most famous woman in America when she arrived in Austerlitz. And she perhaps put Austerlitz on the map in perpetuity for visitors and the world at large when she penned "The Buck in the Snow" by placing her adopted home as the backdrop of this beloved piece. Millay honored the town by announcing her new work, including this famous poem, to the *Chatham Courier* in August 1928. Her inspiration for the new book of collected poems, Millay said, came one night when she saw a giant deer with wonderful antlers wander over the snow near her home in the hills. In return for Millay's taking up residence in their midst, the people of Chatham and Austerlitz showed deep and abiding pride in their world-famous friend.

Millay came down from the mountain frequently and would commune with her neighbors. She was well known throughout Columbia County. In the Millay holdings at Vassar College, there is a version of the poem "Men Working" that is reproduced on several ditto pages. According to the notes in the folder, the ditto copies were mailed to the Vassar College collection by a supervisor of the New York State Electric Corporation in Chatham, New York, in 1954. At the bottom of one of the two ditto copies of the poem, there is the following note: "Presented by Miss Millay to Mr. Fred Munch, Canaan, New York, in July, 1948." Further information in the folder explains that Mr. Munch, with his crew, was constructing the private portion of an extension of electric facilities to serve Steepletop. According to Gladys Taber, Millay had direct contact with a group of utility linemen during the installation of poles and wires that took place in the summer and fall of 1948. On the spot, Taber reported, Millay approached the workmen and read them her poetic efforts:

> *As the last pole was lifted into place Edna showed us a poem which she had written while the men were working high in the air those cool autumn days. She read it aloud to the linemen. It was a cold brilliant day, and the men stood in the clear light by the tall dark pole and listened to Miss Millay's lovely voice. It was the first time, one man said, he had realized that there was beauty in work, his kind of work.*

Millay's fearless voice also appeared in 1929, when the poet made her way into local politics by becoming a member of the Democratic committee in the town of Austerlitz. Papers also reported the time she was stranded in Albany with her husband and a friend without any money and the people of the town came to her aid. Locals heralded the day she and Eugen left for Africa with a front-page story quoting John Haynes Holmes calling Millay the "Greatest Woman Poet since Sappho."

Needless to say Millay was unbridled in her life, yet she was supported by many as she lived a quiet existence in Columbia County. Among those devoted to the internationally celebrated poet were longtime friends George Michael Lucien LaBranche, the renowned fly fisherman, writer and Austerlitz neighbor, and Eugen's best friend, William Brann, who was a summer resident in Austerlitz and a Thoroughbred horse breeder in Maryland.

William Brann (in hat) in the Winner's Circle at the Kentucky Derby with Challedon, 1939. *Courtesy of the Maryland Horse Breeders Association.*

In the late 1930s, just after the infamous crash of the New York stock market, the Boissevains were introduced to the allure of horses and secretly became co-owners of several racehorses with William Brann's help. Millay corresponded with Brann through letters that are now stored in several containers in the Library of Congress, along with a trove of papers donated by Edna's sister, Norma.

Their almost daily correspondence allowed Millay and Brann to miraculously breed a Class A racehorse that Millay named Challedon. Brann also named one of the horses in his stable "the Millay." As a three-year-old, Challedon finished second in the 1939 Kentucky Derby. In the Preakness Stakes, he won and became eligible to run at Belmont. Despite the best training and several hopeful starts, in 1939, her beloved young prospect faltered and failed to win the three most coveted races: the Kentucky Derby, the Preakness and the Belmont Stakes, which today are known as the Triple Crown. Despite this disappointment, Millay wrote "The Ballad of Chaldon Down," a poem about her amazing young steed. After Millay gave up her interest in Challedon, the colt went on to have a profitable career, earning well over $300,000.

Austerlitz

Austerlitz began as an untamed, inhospitable settlement, but Edna St. Vincent Millay's infusion of art amid natural beauty illuminated its rare and magical qualities.

Upon her husband's death, Millay retreated to her home, Steepletop, receiving few visitors for a full year. She relied on her most loyal staff and ventured out infrequently.

Sadly Edna St. Vincent Millay died in the very placed she loved in 1950 as a result of a heart attack. Her sister Norma Millay took up residence at Steepletop soon thereafter. With great respect for her beloved sister's legacy, Norma preserved the house, gardens and grounds exactly the way Edna had left them the day she died.

The *Chatham Courier* reported on Thursday, October 28, 1950, that two devoted women who had worked for the poet climbed the fields behind her house days after her death in search of the beautiful steeplebush that Millay had so loved. Though the season had passed for the blooming pink stems, the women looked endlessly until they found at least one unfaded bloom. They placed the flower in Millay's hands as she lay in her coffin so that something earthly from Austerlitz would be with her always.

Millay's ashes were interred by her sister Norma at Steepletop in a gravesite at the end of a wooded poetry trail on the grounds of the Edna St. Vincent Millay Society in Austerlitz.

2
CHATHAM

HOW DO YOU MAKE A HAMLET?

What makes Chatham so interesting is not necessarily the whole place but the sum of its parts. The town of Chatham is made up of many hamlets. Just for the record, the definition of a hamlet varies from country to country. In the United State, hamlets are a type of settlement with no official boundaries but are often marked by significant road signs. Interestingly, the word *hamlet* has Dutch origins and comes from the word *heemraden*, meaning officials of the Dutch courts. The word *heem*, from which this word is derived, means "homestead" and is connected to a German word meaning a hedge. Meanwhile, *raad* means "councilor." The heemraad were members of the Dyk court whose principal function was to determine boundaries. The term goes back to pre-medieval days. Literally, the term means "home advisor."

The town of Chatham was erected on March 17, 1795, taking about equal portions from Canaan and Kinderhook, and later portions were set off in forming the towns of Ghent and Austerlitz. Its first settlers were Hollanders moving north from Kinderhook, Quakers and later New Englanders. The first town meeting took place at the home of Ebenezor Crocker. The early settlers were William Thomas, who originally owned the greater part of the village site, and Captain Thomas Groat, who settled soon after and whose name was attached to the place as Groat's Corners, until the more appropriate title of Chatham Four Corners came into use, to continue until 1869, when it was called Chatham Village.

Chatham's Main Street, Chatham, New York, early 1900s. *Courtesy of Chatham Historical Society.*

Chatham's famous clock tower, Chatham, New York. *Courtesy of Chatham Historical Society.*

CHATHAM

The Stanwix Hotel/Groats Inn, Chatham, New York. *Courtesy of the Chatham Historical Society.*

It was a lively industrial place mostly because it was the hub for five railway lines, launching over one hundred trains each day to different parts of the Northeast. The mills were very prominent, producing paper and bricks by taking full advantage of power from the cascading creek waters that pass through the town. While some may think that Hudson is the biggest town in the county, Chatham is actually the largest with an area of 31,703 acres. It has eleven hamlets in all.

There is plenty that is hidden in Chatham Village. For instance, the renowned clock tower on Main Street, which looks a lot like a scene from the movie *Back to the Future*, has the only pendulum clock still in its original condition and still working. The 1811 House is the oldest building in town and was frequented by Martin Van Buren, who merrily rode his horse there from Kinderhook.

Mr. William Thomas first built this hotel, calling it Stanwix Hall, in 1811 and moved in with his young bride. The enterprising Mr. Thomas then began the construction of a second tavern, the Park House, which was moved up River Street.

Snake Oil and Snake Charmers

The Park Hotel, originally built in 1815, was visited by Harry Houdini and Teddy Roosevelt. It was later called the Windsor Hotel. It then became the known as the Hygea Sanitarium, which had the express purpose of curing cancer. The Windsor Hotel Sanitarium/ Hygea was a grand building with four stories and fabulous balconies on all sides. Two brothers, C.H. and Abbott Mason, founded the sanitarium in the late 1890s. The Windsor was a curious place from the start. It was a creative enterprise and quite successful, renting rooms to both railroad workers and very sick patients who sought treatment for physical and emotional problems.

Hygea Sanitarium advertisement, Chatham, New York. *Courtesy of the Chatham Historical Society.*

Chatham

In advertisements in the 1800s, Mason medicinals offered a radical cure for cancer and the complete elimination of tumors. According to the ads, one could write to or see C.H. Mason, MD, of Chatham, New York, and could receive advice by mail or a free consultation. A six-week home treatment was only ten dollars and promised "no pain and no knife." The brothers were most well known for their famous "Vegetable Cancer Cure," which they sold by mail, but they preferred that patients be treated at the sanitarium in Chatham. Testimonials were quite frequent, as many patients would report recovering from near death after taking the cure. The sanitarium suffered a great fire, from which all of the occupants but one escaped. This was not the great escape artist, Houdini, who had visited the hotel, but rather a salesman employed by Monarch Books of Philadelphia, Pennsylvania.

If the Spirit Moves You

One of the more unknown hamlets of Chatham is a tiny placed called Rayville. Rayville is situated in the northern part of Chatham between the town New Lebanon to the west and Riders Mills hamlet to the east. In the

Quaker's Picnic portrait taken at Rayville Meetinghouse, Rayville, New York/town of Chatham. *Courtesy of Friends Burial Ground at Rayville.*

Quaker meetinghouse, Rayville, New York/town of Chatham. *Courtesy of Friends Burial Ground at Rayville.*

1750s and '60s, this area was called New Britton and was situated in the King's District, Albany County.

A man by the name of Savage took a grant for this land, which included one thousand acres extending southeast from the Kinderhook Creek. About forty families of the Society of Friends settled here from Nine Partners, one of the original and most important Quaker settlements in Dutchess County, New York. The Great Nine Partners' Patent was granted on May 27, 1697, to Caleb Heathcote and Company and included land covering most of Dutchess County, from the Hudson to the Connecticut line.

Samuel Ray emigrated from Great Britain to Nantucket Island in the early 1700s fleeing religious persecution. His descendant, Nathaniel Ray, was one of the original settlers in Columbia County, and it was Francis Ray who would make his home there and eventually call the hamlet "Rayville" in 1781.

The Quakers were a religious group that originated in England. They rejected the conventional beliefs of the organized Church of England and chose to follow the Bible as the true authority and guide of their religious faith. During the Reformation in the sixteenth and seventeenth centuries, many similar groups emerged. Because of their differences with the Church, the Friends were persecuted, and at one time, four thousand Friends were confined in unsanitary prisons in England, where they eventually died. The Friends first came to America in 1656 and found refuge in Rhode Island.

Friends worshipped in Rayville at gatherings called "meetings," which were void of music, singing and talking. As the meeting progressed, if no one felt that they were called upon by the Holy Spirit to speak or pray, the congregation would simply sit quietly and meditate. When "the spirit moved them," members would speak with a great amount of zeal and passion, and often, they would shake or tremble—thus the name "Quakers." The Friends adopted the English style of separating men and women in their meetings, and they dressed in a plain style. They followed the word of Jesus that all men were created equal and that superiority was given to God only.

First in Hudson and later in Chatham, Elias Hicks was an early Quaker preacher. In his journal, he mentions visiting New Britain (or Britton) in the year 1781, when he met Obediah Wilbur, David Reynolds and Jehiel Palmer at a Friends meetinghouse near the Reynoldses' barn in Rayville.

The Friends who gathered here built a simple log meetinghouse near the Green Brook on the eastern side of the current Rayville Burial ground. Many deeds in the hamlet today identify land parameters with reference to a particular number of "rods" and "yards" measured from the Friends' meetinghouse.

The Quakers of Rayville prospered until 1805 when their preacher died and was replaced by Daniel Haight. The group then outgrew its log

Quaker member initials carved on the wall of the Rayville Meetinghouse, Rayville, New York/town of Chatham. *Photo by Bob Balcum, courtesy of Friends Burial Ground at Rayville.*

meetinghouse and built a larger space. Haight carried the congregation ministry until 1813, when he died and was replace by Henry Post until 1824, when Ruth Mosher continued the work. After Mosher another woman, Mary Gardner, preached until 1837. Later, the society was served by Thomas Rider, and then his daughter Mary Hudson took over. In the late 1800s, the Quakers of Rayville were still active. The Society of Friends at Rayville endured for over 160 years.

Quakers Standing Up for Slaves

Among many remarkable qualities, Quakers were staunch supporters of equality and elevated women to the highest positions. The Rayville Quakers also created a school and poorhouse to care for the elderly and others who were interned or handicapped. It was also no secret that they opposed slavery. In 1793, the United States passed the first Fugitive Slave Law, making it illegal to help a slave escape or to give shelter to a runaway slave. A fine of $500 was issued under this law. While the practice of slavery was being ended in many places in the world, the United States was determined to continue it. As a group, Quakers were the first to speak out against slavery in America. The Philadelphia Abolition Society, a Quaker organization with Benjamin Franklin as a leading member, had been established in 1775. One of the first organized slave escapes took place in Virginia in 1786 with assistance from Quakers.

While many believe that slavery was contained in the South, in fact, New York had the largest number of slaves in the North, and it is clear that the Hudson Valley was one of the main routes for the Underground Railroad, an organized system for transporting fugitive slaves. Not surprisingly, though thousands of slaves traveled the route from Pennsylvania to Vermont, passing directly through Columbia County, no one knows exactly how they did it. What is known is that they were aided by free blacks and Quakers via a string of Quaker communities from New York to Burlington, as documented in a letter written by Roland Robinson, which is available at the Rokeby Museum, the underground site just south of Burlington, Vermont. Robinson was a close friend of Isaac T. Hopper and other committed Quaker abolitionists. He wrote that one could travel in Quaker meeting places at Nine Partners, Pleasant Valley, Poughkeepsie and Crum Elbow near Hyde Park in Dutchess County; Claverack, Hudson, Ghent and Chatham in Columbia County; and Troy.

Chatham

There are similar accounts of houses in Ghent and Chatham being used by the Underground Railroad to harbor escaped slaves written by Dr. William Cady Bailey, a relative of Elizabeth Cady Stanton.

Aaron Powell, a Quaker from Chatham, was a prominent antislavery advocate. On the Powell farm in Ghent near Arnold's Mill was an old 1795 Quaker meetinghouse. In the house was a secret cellar. It is in that same house where Charles Van Buren—whose grandfather, George, was a slave at the home of Martin Van Buren, who would later become president—wrote of his early recollections of terrified slaves escaping cruel masters and being chased by bloodhounds. The Quaker meetinghouse reportedly had a concrete cellar where the slaves, mostly fleeing the South, were hidden. Powell was also famous for protesting against marriage inequality in 1861. In that time laws were written in such a way that women would relinquish their possessions upon marriage, rendering a wife inferior to her husband and removing her individuality.

The Powell name lives on with a Quaker meetinghouse, which was erected on land donated by descendant Elise Powell, which is still active in Old Chatham today.

Painting the Town Red

In the long list of Chatham hamlets, hidden history abounds in the little hamlet of East Chatham near the western side of town not far from Austerlitz called Red Rock. It's a sleepy place mapped on crooked back roads that lead to a cluster of historic houses. The hamlet borders are crafted in a way that suggests that Red Rock may also sit partly in Canaan.

Red Rock is actually one of the oldest settlements in Columbia County. It is nestled into the Austerlitz hills along the winding outline of the Indian Creek. It was here, by the creek and in the country meadows, that the Stockbridge Indians made camp, lived peacefully and, according to many accounts, wove spectacular willow baskets that they hung from trees like decorative holiday ornaments.

In the early days when the settlement began, about 1756, it was a tiny place with a lot of activity. At the beginning, it held three churches, a sawmill, a gristmill and thirty dwellings. There are reports that suggest that two families of Shakers, consisting of about seventy-five people, resided in the northeastern part of the town (most likely what is now Canaan). At a meeting

Red Rock Obelisk, Red Rock, New York/town of Chatham. *Collection of Jon and April Meredith, Kinderhook, New York.*

of the citizens of "Kings District" on June 24, 1776, delegates were chosen, and among the early families were the names Douglass, Warner, Whiting, Alesworth, Baldwin and Hawley. The first mill was built by Wm. B. Whiting, about 1775. This mill, stored with grain belonging to the government, was

Chatham

People of Red Rock gather for a public auction in the late 1800s, Red Rock, New York/town of Chatham. *Collection of Jon and April Meredith, Kinderhook, New York.*

Ford's Store, Red Rock, New York/town of Chatham. *Collection of Jon and April Meredith, Kinderhook, New York.*

burned by Tories during the Revolutionary War. In the first book of records is a memorandum, without a date or signature, suggesting that the town records were kept on loose paper previous to 1772. The land sale deed from the Indians of six square miles was executed in 1758. The compensation at the time of the sale was £250.

Of the first pioneers who traveled west in wagons over the Berkshire Hills of Massachusetts and the hills of Connecticut were the Fords. With an ox cart pulling the family and possessions, the Fords reportedly passed the many campfires of the Stockbridge Indians by the creek and made their way to a clearing where they eventually built their home. Legend has it that the natives would frequently visit the brick Ford house in search of "muckymuck," or a word that sounded much like that, which the settlers thought stood for "meat." Yet in many definitions, Muckamuck really means a person of importance. It is quite possible that the Native Americans had really been looking for the white man's chief rather than food.

The former name of the hamlet, Pilfershire, naturally draws you in and asks the question, why Pilfershire? As the story goes, before it was officially the hamlet of Red Rock, it was a mere settlement and part of the western slope of the Berkshire Hills. According to a piece written by Mary Y. Patterson in 1901 in the September *Ladies' Home Journal*, "Twenty-five years before the battle of Lexington, in 1750, Sylvanus Cunningham, a peddler of notions, passed through the settlement. His horse spooked, and his cart was upset and all of his wares thrown out into the road. The villagers rushed to his aid, but when he took a hasty inventory of his stock, he declared that much was missing and furthermore denounced the place, saying it should thenceforth be known as Pilfershire."

And so the name stuck until finally, in 1825, when the village elders got together to get rid of the humiliating name. (There's actually an abandoned village called Pilfershire in Simsbury, Connecticut, with a mysterious past—for another book I guess.) The townspeople started to suggest names to replace the embarrassing name. One member of the group called out "Red Rock." Soon there were objections since no one felt confident that there were any "red rocks" in the vicinity; however, the gathering solved the problem by locating a huge rock and covering it with a thick, deep coat of red paint! Since then, about every twelve or so years, the town celebrates "painting day," when the rock gets spruced up with a fresh coat of barn paint.

In winter, when the snows made roads impassable, Red Rock was almost completely cut off from the rest of the world. Months of restlessness, stale menus and the depletion of maple syrup caused many in the town to send one of its own young men to "drive a yoke of Oxen" to Boston for a barrel of molasses. As if being sent to war, his mother begged him not to go. Yet

Elizabeth Cady Stanton (seated) with Susan B. Anthony (standing). Courtesy of the Library of Congress.

over the Berkshires he went with his team, and three months later returned with a "hogs head" of molasses for the town.

In the same neighborhood, as early as 1760, Eleazor Cady settled. Eleazor had a brother, Elijah, whose wife, Isabel Jackson, was a cousin of President Andrew

Jackson. One of Eleazor's sons, Daniel Cady, was the father of Elizabeth Cady Stanton, who was born in New Concord right next door to Red Rock in 1815.

Cady was known nationally as a famous suffragette and was also a social activist and abolitionist, and she is often credited with the first women's rights and women's suffrage movements in the United States. A somewhat less known fact about Cady was that she supported the temperance movement, which generally aimed at curbing the consumption of alcohol, which many felt contributed greatly to spousal abuse. Stanton is a leading figure of the early women's movement, presenting her "Declaration of Sentiments" at the first women's rights convention in Seneca Falls in 1848, which she organized.

Take to the Lake

Has this history been forgotten, whisked away by time or simply dried up? Kinderhook Lake is one of Chatham's more unusual places.

Today, as you drive down Route 203 past Kinderhook Lake, you might only see a pretty oversized pond, but in the early 1900s, it was the destination of thousands of visitors. Of all the lakes in New York State, Kinderhook Lake has the unique distinction of having been one of the first to be electrified.

Electric Park trolley lets off passengers at Kinderhook Lake in the early 1900s. *Collection of Jon and April Meredith, Kinderhook, New York.*

With a brilliant idea to increase the use of the rail line trolleys, the Albany/Hudson Railway, the first rural electric trolley line in the country, built a huge amusement park on Kinderhook Lake.

Electric Park was the somewhat sensible name chosen to identify this amazing destination and other parks like it that were built in the United States and operated by accessing the trolley line's electric current. It was promoted as safe and fun. It was also designed to be affordable. For the price of a trolley ride, travelers from as far away as Boston could enjoy the park for just five cents and ride the steam powered Ferris wheel, which was located outside the gates. If you traveled by train and paid the forty cents for round-trip fare, you got in for free. Unlike today's water slide worlds, this park was running year-round. On a huge wooden slide called the Chute-the-Chute, those with ice in their veins could ride a summer float onto the frozen lake or board a winter toboggan and slide along the snow-covered ice. Winter also offered skating, curling and dancing.

Electric Park was the largest amusement park said to be operating in the early 1900s between New York City and Montreal, and in summer, it was humming. The entire lake was decorated with colorful lights, giving off a spectacular reflection on the calm lake waters. Parkgoers could ride a roller coaster over the water of a lagoon near the entrance with a carousel on a small island in the center of the lagoon.

Electric Park Ferris wheel at Kinderhook Lake in the early 1900s. *Collection of Jon and April Meredith, Kinderhook, New York.*

HIDDEN HISTORY OF COLUMBIA COUNTY, NEW YORK

Electric Park Chute-the-Chute water slide at Kinderhook Lake in the early 1900s. *Collection of Jon and April Meredith, Kinderhook, New York.*

Electric Park sign. *Collection of Jon and April Meredith, Kinderhook, New York.*

There was an active Pony Track, and snacks, such as popcorn, candy, soda pop, ice cream and roasted peanuts, were sold to hungry patrons. To get anything more potent to drink, since the park was resting on Chatham's "dry" zone, one had to rent a paddleboat and cruise to Hawley Point, one of two islands within the lake known as "rest areas," as is recorded on the Kinderhook Lake Corporation's website.

Later, a rickety wooden bridge was constructed by breaking through the frozen lake water to create easier access. A dance hall, restaurant, bowling alley, shooting gallery and theater were also part of the fun. There were two performances each day at the theater for plays, vaudeville shows and, later, movies.

To increase attendance, ads ran in the *Chatham Courier* for the park and noted some remarkable performances to be witnessed. In one ad was the description of the astonishing Professor Joe D'Amica, who could play the violin behind his back, over his head and in a hundred different positions. He would also play charming and enchanting music on a tomato-can violin with only one string. The ad continued to promote the talent of another professor, Guarieri of Philadelphia, who could offer the best sleight-of-hand and pleasing tricks; a woman without a body who could drink water; and a New York troupe offering plantation songs, Irish music, clog ballet and fancy dancing. Last but not least, it told of the appearance of an ossified man who hadn't moved in twenty-six years.

But this park would never have been put on the map if it had not been for Charles Delemere Haines. Charles D. and his brothers established the original Kinderhook Lake Park thirty years before Electric Park, as a place for people to meet, picnic, play games and fish.

He was originally from Medusa in Albany County, New York, and as an aspiring young entrepreneur, he became a telegrapher in the office of the NYC&HR Railroad in Hudson at the age of sixteen and rapidly became a train dispatcher and then assistant superintendent. With the help of his brothers, he established the Haines Brothers firm in Kinderhook and New York City and, by 1898, held a controlling interest in the Kinderhook & Hudson Railroad and controlled at least a dozen other railroad companies, including the Lebanon Springs Railroad, along with the Great Columbian Hall Hotel and Resort at Lebanon Springs (more about this in the New Lebanon chapter). He would later become a U.S. congressman, elected to represent New York's Nineteenth District in the U.S. House of Representatives, serving from 1893 to 1895, being defeated in 1896.

By the time the new owners were surveying the old park for purchase to build the new Electric Park, it had been severely vandalized.

Eventually, World War I and the development of the automobile put an end to the renowned Electric Park as a unique attraction. It closed in 1915 and attempts were made to reopen in 1917, but they failed. It closed for good in 1921.

He Knows What Flows

Hidden underground, unseen and unheard, are an abundance of waterways. Finding water is both an art and a science. Water is vital to all communities, and toward the latter part of the 1960s, residents of Columbia County worried that water supplies might be drying up. Rather than engaging in expensive drilling, the townspeople turned to a special group of individuals belonging to the American Society of Dowsers, which is a group of men and women who are blessed with the amazing power of locating water underground. While most myths and movies portray old dowsers in the desert with twigs and branches in their hands, the truth is that dowsers use a number of strange objects to locate underground aquifers, including chains, forked willow branches and wands. Dowsing is a technique that traces back in history to the Bible, and perhaps because these people were given these special gifts, dowsers did not accept money for their services.

Back in the day, Marcel Triau, a French immigrant who lived in Columbia County, possessed extra-sensory powers and was known as the local dowsing expert. Triau reported that he would have a certain feeling come over him when he felt that water was near. He said he learned to know this feeling from another dowser who visited his family farm when he was a child.

By day, Mr. Triau ran the gas station on the very eastern edge of Chatham in Canaan, New York, on the corner of Routes 22 and 295, just north of Austerlitz. When not at the station, Mr. Triau was finding water. One of his best finds was a three-hundred-gallon-per-minute flow that was used to service over one hundred homes in Chatham. Mr. Triau also predicted that a large underground system of water could be found under Chatham's Birge Hill Road in East Chatham, and a mighty underground river flowed not far from that location that cut diagonally across the village of Chatham.

The supernatural technique employed by Mr. Triau and others was fairly simple. When searching for water, he would point his left arm straight out and then twirl a small chain in his right hand. In doing this, he allowed his subconscious mind to receive a silent message. Though there are doubters of the dowsers, the truth is told in the statistics. Mr. Triau's abilities were 97 percent accurate.

Chatham

What's in a Game?

As Chatham has historically been a quiet town with agriculture at its roots, its list of truly bizarre events is a short one. So when seventeen-year-old Wyley Gates shot his father, his brother, his three-year-old cousin and his father's live-in girlfriend in cold blood on a chilly December night in 1986 at their East Chatham home, it left the place shocked, stunned and scared. What was even more disturbing to neighbors and classmates of the Chatham High School senior was that it appeared to be a fully planned assassination, as evidenced on a computer stolen from the school and the execution-style murders committed with a gun stolen from his family home.

On December 13, Wyley's grandmother Vivian Gates made a frantic call to police explaining that her grandson had just discovered the four dead bodies in his home at Maple Drive. The police immediately sent out bulletins that a killer might be on the loose. Despite the panic of his grandmother and police, Wyley apparently sat in his grandmother's kitchen calmly explaining that they were all dead.

When authorities arrived at the Gateses' log cabin home, they were horrified to find that each victim had been shot a number of times, with up to twenty bullets being used in the murder. The police questioned Wyley, who said he had last seen his family the night before going to the Crandell Theater to see a Clint Eastwood movie with friends. Under intense questioning, Wyley finally made incriminating mistakes in his story that led the police to arrest him. The investigation uncovered the strange and unexpected reality that Wyley and friends had been taking part in a role-playing game based on the popular Dungeons and Dragons. They say it was called Infierno, which in Spanish means "hell." In this case, Wyley's crime plan was found on the school computer. The police were so convinced of his guilt that they barely collected any evidence. The lack of quality police work ultimately undermined the case, and Gates was acquitted of murder but found guilty of conspiracy and sent to prison. The bizarre story doesn't end there. In 2003, though he finally confessed to killing his family, Wyley Gates walked out of prison with a college degree, heading for New York City. He had served seventeen years in prison and was paroled. With his new degree, he secured an apartment and a job with a law firm. Today, Gates's whereabouts are unknown.

3
CLAVERACK

Where Dinosaurs Roamed

Claverack is Dutch for "clover reach." Some accounts say that it was Henry Hudson's sighting of vast fields of white clover that inspired the name. Other stories are told of those who traveled the river from New Amsterdam (New York City) north, dividing their journeys into *raks*, or "reaches," a distance that a ship could sail in a day.

The Dutch were the first European explorers to inhabit the Hudson River Valley in search of fur trade routes. To protect their interests from the ever-encroaching British, the Dutch royal crown sold large parcels of land to wealthy men who were given a patroonship or manors. These patroons, in return for the land, promised to populate it as a way of ensuring Dutch domain over New Netherlands.

In 1630, Killian Van Rensselaer, a diamond merchant and one of the original directors of the Dutch West India Company (Henry Hudson's employers), purchased the largest of the patroonships—*Rensselaerwyck*. Most of his holdings were near Fort Orange (present-day Albany), but 170,000 acres were located below Kinderhook along the east bank of the Hudson River. In 1704, Killian gave his brother, Hendrick, all 170,000 acres, some of which belonged to the Native Americans and was land they originally called "Pot Koke."

Claverack is one of the original divisions of Columbia County formed in 1772. It encompassed parts of Albany, all that was south of Kinderhook

Hidden History of Columbia County, New York

Skyline view from Claverack, New York, looking out over the Catskill Mountains and toward the Hudson River. *Taken by the author, October 2013.*

Kiliaen Van Rensselaer, head-and-shoulders portrait/engraving, facing left by Charles Balthazar Julien Fevret de Saint-Memin, 1805. *Courtesy of the Library of Congress.*

and Livingston Manor, which was then part of Dutchess County. In 1782, Hillsdale was taken off, and everything west of Claverack Creek became the city of Hudson, formerly Claverack Landing. By 1788, it had become a town and then was further reduced when the town of Ghent was erected in 1818.

Claverack sits in the shadow of the blue mountain Catskills, where Irving's Rip Van Winkle was born, and in Claverack, Clement Moore's poem "The Night Before Christmas" was written at the home of his friend James Watson Webb. Yet Claverack has another history. Some ten thousand years ago, during the Pleistocene era, Columbia County was covered in ice, and mastodons freely roamed the region.

In 1705, Cotton Mather, known widely in witchcraft circles, had been generally credited, incorrectly, with the first printed account of the discovery of mastodon remains in Claverack. As it turned out, the discovery was indeed the first major fossil found by colonists, but it was not exactly made by Mather.

In a letter to Dr. Woodward of England, dated November 17, 1712, and published in the *Philosophical Transactions of the Royal Society of London* for 1714, Mather described the find briefly: "Bones and teeth of some large animals found lately in New England." Giving a literal interpretation of the biblical statement "there were giants in the earth in those days," Mather judged the remains to be of "ante diluvial giant men...sold to Van Bruggen for a gill of rum."

In reality, the information came from a letter Mather received from Governor Joseph Dudley dated July 10, 1705, from a story that was first published in a Boston newsletter, which described the discovery of a tooth, weighing about four pounds and three quarters "with a fang that could hold about a half pint of liquor." The article goes on to say how, in Claverack, the tooth rolled down a hill about thirty or forty feet. Digging on the site where the tooth landed uncovered a seventeen-foot-long thighbone and other parts of the unidentified animal that, when unearthed, immediately crumbled away. The early excavators also dug up another tooth and reportedly some massive trees. This information, originally credited to the Royal Society of London, actually came from Dunlap's *History of New Netherlands*. It seems it was hard keeping track of such things back then.

Claverack is now credited with the discovery of the first mammut or mammoth, which became known as the "Incognitum." It wasn't until much later, when similar remains turned up in South Carolina, that slaves connected the bones to the shape of the African elephant, and it became

Mastodon tooth in the Buffalo Museum of Science. *Courtesy of the Library of Congress.*

clear that the animal they found was related. There have been more than one hundred mastodon and mammoth remains recovered in New York State, more than half from the Hudson Valley (mostly in Orange County).

THE LAW OF THE LAND

By 1786, Claverack was the first "seat" of the state, or the administrative center where the governing functions convened. Naturally, there were then

CLAVERACK

Alexander Hamilton painting by John Trumbell. *Courtesy of the Library of Congress.*

lots of lawyers and famous cases, and so Claverack built the county's very first courthouse. Over 3,600 English pounds were spent to construct the Federal-style brick structure with a large courtroom on the second floor and a jail facility in the back. The building was opened in 1789 and became the scene for many significant judicial debates.

The most significant of these cases was the well-publicized libel trial that positioned President Thomas Jefferson against Federalist newspaper editor Harry Croswell. Though he was convicted of libel at Claverack, in a landmark appeals case argued by Alexander Hamilton, the conviction was overturned. Alexander Hamilton was already fairly well known in Columbia County. He formed an artillery company in 1775 and at age twenty, he became George Washington's confidential assistant or aide-de-camp. After the Revolution, Hamilton helped lead the efforts to create a constitutional convention and served as the first Secretary of the Treasury under President Washington.

This leads us to even more interesting history in Claverack. During the Revolution, Aaron Burr was with Benedict Arnold during an attempted invasion of Canada. He also wintered with Washington at Valley Forge. Later, in races for president of the United States and governor of New York, Aaron Burr was defeated, in part due to the efforts of Alexander Hamilton, which led to their growing hatred for each other. This eventually led to the famous duel in 1804 in which Hamilton was killed. The duel reportedly took place at the Claverack courthouse.

In the early part of the nineteenth century, Alexander Hamilton's fame was widespread, and the achievements of his brilliant intellect and honorable political career were acknowledged by all, even by those politically antagonistic to him. The tragic ending of the duel between Hamilton and Burr has cast a shadow over Burr's memory, but few remember that in many of the acts of his life, he was heroic and patriotic and used his great talents for what he deemed to be the good of his country.

Following the removal of the "seat of justice" to Hudson, the Claverack courthouse passed through various uses, being utilized both as a school and a hall for social gatherings. After several years, the building was transformed into an attractive and spacious residence, the home of Mr. Peter Hoffman. Yet under the summerhouse in the garden, there once was a dungeon where criminals were confined. At the east of the courthouse stood the jail and pillory and an old whipping post was prominent in the cellar.

Hangman's Tree

The Claverack courthouse was also the site of the eerie hangman's tree. At the rear of the courthouse, there was a large maple with thick limbs where more than twelve men and one woman wore the noose. The most infamous case was that of a baby's nurse named Peggy Densmore. In the 1780s, Peggy was hired by a prominent Claverack family to care for their infant daughter. When the child suddenly died, the courts convicted Peggy of murder and sentenced her to hang. As she made her way toward the big tree, Peggy grasped a delicate hanky in her hand and remarked that if, while she was hanging, the hanky slipped from her hand, then she was guilty, but if it remained in her grasp, then she was innocent. Apparently, the hanky never fell to the earth the day that Peggy was hanged, and several years later, the mother of the baby confessed to poisoning her own child.

The tree at the courthouse saw another gruesome hanging when Joseph Brown was executed there for the murder of a child. On December 5, 1867, Josephine and Joseph Brown were indicted for the murder of Angeline Stewart. This horrific story involves a couple from Canaan, New York, who adopted—some say kidnapped—Angeline, who lived with her family in Dayton, Ohio. The girl came to live with the couple after her destitute mother seemingly gave her away.

One night, while Mrs. Brown was visiting neighbors in Chatham, Mr. Brown murdered the young girl and set the house aflame. The apparent motive was a $5,000 life insurance policy taken out on the young lady by her new parents just weeks prior. In hopes of saving herself, Josephine Brown implicated her husband, Joseph.

The actions that led to the murder included a chain of lies and deceit, including a fabricated marriage, abduction and insurance fraud. Suspicious details revealed by the insurance company investigator indicated that little Angie had not inhaled smoke, thus proving the girl was dead before the fire occurred. The victim was found in the basement of the house, and during the trial, diagrams described the space she inhabited as just twenty-seven square feet with only one small window. Apparently Brown had secured a short-term lease to live in the basement with his new family, and it was rumored that he held the girl as a prisoner there.

The lawyer for the prosecution laid out a case that accused both Joseph and Josephine Brown of plotting the murder from the day they arrived in Dayton, Ohio, until the day of Angelina's death. He proved that their eagerness to obtain the insurance money and their indifference at Angelina's burial were traits indicative of individuals with a "hateful heart." Joseph Brown was held for some time before he was hanged, and his wife, Josephine, ended up being acquitted.

True-Blue Traitor

But let's not leave Benedict Arnold out of the early accounts of Claverack's hidden history. If you search any text about Benedict Arnold, you'll be

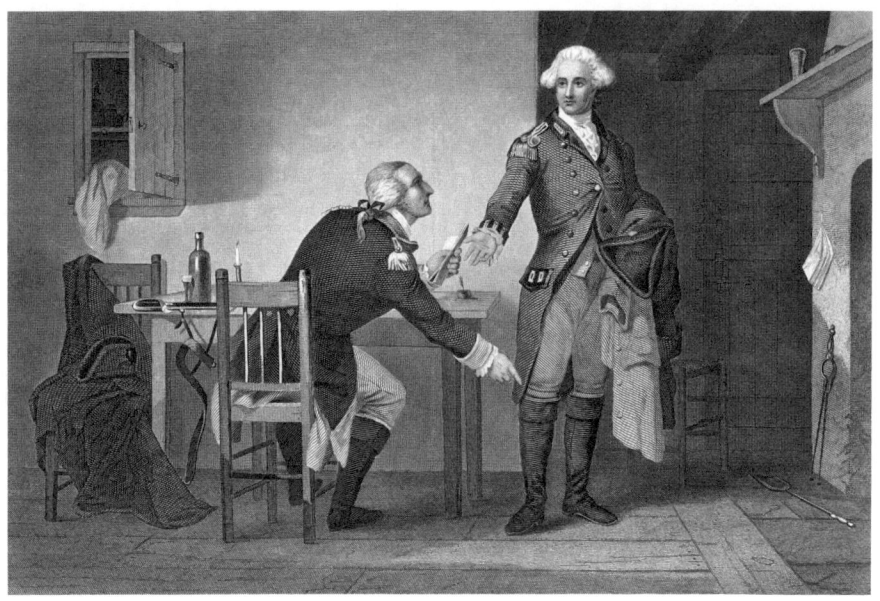

Treason of Arnold Persuades Andre to Conceal Papers in His Boot, etching by C.F. Blauvelt, 1847. *Courtesy of the Library of Congress.*

surprised to find that he was described in a number of ways: handsome, brave, smart. Yet turncoat seems to be the one adjective that stuck.

Arnold served his country by fighting the French at Lake George as part of the Connecticut militia in the mid-1700s and fought in the Revolution, during which he was wounded fairly badly. In fact, the Benedict Arnold House in the center of Kinderhook, New York, is supposedly where Arnold was taken after being wounded in the Battle of Beemis Heights. The fact remains, sadly, that he was never recognized and never rewarded and, as a result, became outraged and rebellious.

Arnold lost the trust of his peers and commanders with reckless behavior. His anger and his own feelings of betrayal caused him to eventually defect to the British army and enter into secret negotiations, turning West Point over to the British. Yet his plot failed when his accomplice, Major Andre, was captured. When he discovered the news of the betrayal, General Washington requested that Arnold be exchanged for Andre. His captors refused, and Andre was hanged. Arnold narrowly escaped pursuit by Washington through New York, and in 1781, the British gave Arnold a brigadier general's commission with a hefty salary and pension. He eventually died in London on December 3, 1801.

Claverack

A Slave Sues for Freedom

Strange and shocking cases continue in Claverack with a slave by the name of Elizabeth Freeman, who sued for her freedom and won. Freeman was born into slavery about 1742 at the farm of Pieter Hogeboom in Claverack, New York, where she was given the name Bett. When Hogeboom's daughter Hannah married John Ashley of Sheffield, Massachusetts, he gave the newlyweds Bett, who was barely a teenager. She remained with them until

Mum Bett, Jacqueline Rogers illustration for *A Free Woman on God's Earth* written by Jana Laiz and Ann-Elizabeth Barnes. *Courtesy of Crowflies Press.*

1781, during which time she married and had a daughter named Betsy. Her husband (whose name is unknown because Bett was illiterate) never returned from service in the Revolutionary War. One day, Hannah Ashley attempted to strike Bett's daughter with a heated shovel. Bett raised her arm in an attempt to protect her child and in the process received a hideous blow. In an act of silent protest, Bett left the wound in plain site so that visitors could see what her mistress had done to her.

Soon after the incident, Bett had an opportunity to hear the Declaration of Independence being read at her master's home, and it gave her the courage to seek counsel from Theodore Sedgwick to sue for her freedom in court. Sedgwick remarkably took the case and enlisted the aid of Tapping Reeve, the founder of America's first law school, located in Litchfield, Connecticut.

According to Bett's own words, she said, "I heard that paper read yesterday, that says, all men are created equal, and that every man has a right to freedom. I'm not a dumb critter; won't the law give me my freedom?" The case of *Brom and Bett v. Ashley* was heard in August 1781 before the County Court of Common Pleas in Great Barrington, Massachusetts, not far from Claverack.

When the jury ruled in Bett's favor, she became the first African American woman to be set free under the Massachusetts state constitution. The decision in the case of Elizabeth Freeman was cited as a precedent when the Massachusetts Supreme Judicial Court heard the appeal of *Quock Walker v. Jennison* and Walker's freedom was upheld. These cases set the legal precedents that ended slavery in Massachusetts. Bett died in December 1829 and was buried in the Sedgwick family plot in nearby Stockbridge, Massachusetts.

School Days

Just up the road from the Claverack courthouse was the Claverack College/Washington Seminary. It began in 1777, a year after the signing of the Declaration of Independence, as more or less a military-style high school run by the pastor of Claverack's Dutch Reformed church, the Reverend Dr. Gebhard.

The school served up to one hundred students at one time. The trustees, David Sherts and Peter Mesick, contributed a large amount of money to the school. Students came from Albany and Rhinebeck, and Claverack's prominent families sent their children there to be educated in Latin and Greek.

Claverack College view. *Courtesy of Columbia County Historical Society, Kinderhook, New York.*

Claverack College scene. *Courtesy of the Columbia County Historical Society, Kinderhook, New York.*

One young student was Stephen Crane. As an effort to provide Crane with a more stable and disciplined environment, his mother sent him to Claverack College. There were rumors that Crane was involved in episodes of hazing that caused him to transfer schools. Crane's mother negotiated tuition at

$165 per year at Claverack, well under the $225 advertised in the school's catalog. From afar, his mother worried about a selection of roommates, and she encouraged Crane to pursue horseback riding, baseball and tennis. In R.W. Stallman's biography of Crane, Stallman says that Crane took his pony, Pudgy, to Claverack College with him.

Crane was generally successful at military school, and he had a dream of entering West Point, though he would eventually leave without receiving a degree. Crane reluctantly transferred to Lafayette College at the urging of his brother, William, to pursue a more practical career in engineering.

He did, however, love Claverack's martial environment. He later called his time at Claverack "the happiest period of my life." Though he often skipped classes to play baseball, Crane seemed to take the school's military style seriously. He was particularly interested in the uniforms and titles that were bestowed on young men in a military school's culture.

Crane is known for having a lifelong interest in war stories, though he grew up during one of America's more peaceful times. The Civil War had ended in 1865, and the start of the Spanish-American War wouldn't come until 1898. Despite this, it's likely that Crane might have identified strongly with Henry Fleming, the protagonist of *The Red Badge of Courage*, who believes that "there was a portion of the world's history which he had regarded as the time of wars, but it, he thought, had been long gone over the horizon and had disappeared forever." Crane's understanding of war may have come from stories of the war that his father's generation had waged. Crane's military experience merely consisted of adding stripes and medals to his dress uniform and of the clean, orderly rituals of a military school in Claverack.

In 1830, the school became the Claverack Academy, and in 1854, the Claverack College and Hudson River Institute were opened. In 1869, the institution began admitting women.

Yoga of the 1800s: Delsartes

It was the practice of the Claverack College, also known as the Hudson River Institute, in the latter part of the 1800s to perform unusual recitals of Delsartes. The term comes from a French gentleman, François Delsarte, who created a system of acting that utilizes dramatic poses that simulated human emotions. It was often seen in early silent films and was slightly ridiculous. However, it proved later to be an inspiration

CLAVERACK

Claverack College ladies' exercise class in Delsarte. *Courtesy of Columbia County Historical Society, Kinderhook, New York.*

for Isadora Duncan, Ruth St. Dennis and the entire Denishawn School, which included students Martha Graham, Doris Humphrey and Charles Weidman, and thereby, the entire first and second generations of modern dancers. It was studied by Rudolph von Laban and taught by F. Mathias Alexander before they developed their own methods. It was the method used to establish the first acting school in America.

Delsarte's work was praised by some of the greatest minds of the day, from scientists to religious scholars, musicians to artists. Even renowned yogis mentioned it with the greatest respect. In 1871, a student of Delsarte, Steele Mackaye, brought the method to the United States when he moved close to Hudson, New York. The movement exploded. In 1885, a student of Mackaye's, Genevieve Stebbins, wrote a book, *The Delsarte System of Expression*. From there, Delsartes spread even faster, and soon, there were Desartians everywhere. The popularity could be compared to the immense expansion of yoga in the United States today.

The recitals at Claverack College consisted of the women of the school in loose-fitting clothing reading poetry while others draped themselves into various positions expressing the emotions and sentiments of the verses.

Geronimo Is Captured

Another member of the Hudson River Institute and Claverack College characters was John Clum, the Apache agent responsible for capturing Geronimo.

John Clum was born in 1871 on a Claverack farm to William Henry and Elizabeth van Deusen Clum, two Dutch and German descendants. He pursued a classical education at Claverack College and attended the local Dutch Reform Church. He later went to Rutgers, where a rigorous athletic career left him ill. He eventually returned to Claverack and his family's farm. It was there that he read a newspaper story that the federal War Department in Washington, D.C., was organizing a meteorological service. He applied, was accepted and was deployed to Santa Fe, New Mexico, as a weather observer.

When the U.S. government gave the Dutch Reformed Church the charge of the San Carlos Apache Reservation after discovering abuses, it sought out someone at Rutgers to help reorganize, and this created the link to Clum.

Clum recognized the corruption in the system early on with agents pocketing federal money along with supplies designated to house and feed the Apaches. The government soldiers also were killing the Apaches for sport. John Clum arrived at the San Carlos Reservation on Tuesday, August 4, 1874. The very next day, Apache scouts presented him with the severed head of Cochinay, a Tonto Apache renegade they had tracked down and killed. It was apparent that he had inherited a legacy of violence and cruelty, and a military presence that showed both anger toward the Indians and disregard for Indian agents.

Contributing to the problem were politicians in Washington, D.C., who melded all Indians into one group. They did not bother to note the difference between individual tribes, ancient cultures, sacred customs and distinctive languages. They also ignored prior political differences and military alliances. They homogenized their solutions to the "Indian problem" the same way they homogenized the Native People. As a result, friends and foes alike were forced to live in close proximity to one another, and violence was a constant problem.

Clum's approach was radically different. During his tenure at San Carlos, he treated the Apaches as friends, established the first Indian Tribal Police and a Tribal Court, forming a system of Indian self-rule. The Apaches nicknamed him Nantan Betunnikiyeh—*nantan*, meaning "boss" or "leader"; *betunnykahyeh*, meaning "high-forehead." Roughly translated, the phrase meant "Boss with the High Forehead," referring to his baldness. Clum encouraged them to take up the peaceful pursuits of farming and raising cattle.

U.S. Post Office inspecter John Clum on a route to Alaska, 1898. *Courtesy of the Library of Congress.*

The army disliked Clum's actions, as it prevented them from stealing part of the funds that passed through the reservation. Clum tired of the army's constant meddling in his management of the reservation and the lack of support from the Indian Bureau, the very people who sought him out specifically as a man who would make a reputable and effective agent.

Then in September 1872, Cochise peacefully negotiated a reservation for his people in the Dragoon Mountains on the west to the Peloncillo Mountains on the east. It included the Chiricahua Mountains and ran south to the Mexican border. Some members of the tribe continued raids into the Mexican states of Sonora and Chihuahua. The government tried to force them to relocate the reservation, but they lost ground when Cochise died on June 8, 1874.

Seeing trouble on the horizon, on May 3, 1876, the government ordered Clum to transfer the Chiricahuas to San Carlos. After waiting in vain for military reinforcements to help with the move, Clum began relocating the tribe to the best of his ability in early June. Cochise's sons Taza and Naiche agreed to the move and killed several Chircahuas, including Eskinya, Cochise's trusted ally, when he insisted they go to war. The Nednhi Chirica led by Juh also requested transfer. Clum granted them three days to round up their men. They used that time to outwit the cavalry and escape to the south. Of the more than 1,000 Chiricahuas moving, only 42 men and 280 women and children accompanied Clum north.

In April 1877, the Department of the Interior ordered Clum to remove the bands at Ojo Caliente to San Carlos. Victorio and the Chihenne Chiricahuas agreed with the plan at first.

Geronimo was a Bedonkohe Apache who fought against Mexico and the United States over their expansion into Apache tribal lands for several decades. Geronimo was avenging the death of his mother, wife and three children, whom the Mexicans had killed. He was defiant against the government's demands that they move to new territory. It was Clum who hid one hundred of his Apache police in the commissary building at Ojo Caliente and, on April 21, 1877, surprised Geronimo, seizing his rifle and throwing him in chains. His success gave the U.S. Army a black eye. It was the only time Geronimo was captured at gunpoint without a shot fired on either side. Some reports say that Geronimo surrendered under specific conditions, which he later reported were ignored.

Clum and his wife moved to Arizona and bought the *Arizona Citizen*, in which he regularly criticized Washington in editorials. Following the great silver strike in Tombstone in 1877, Clum moved to Tombstone and began publication, on Saturday, May 1, 1880, of the *Tombstone Epitaph*. He helped organize a Vigilance Committee to end lawlessness in Tombstone, and his association with that group helped get him elected as Tombstone's first mayor in 1881. While mayor, he became lifelong friends with Wyatt Earp and became one of his greatest supporters.

BIRTH CONTROL IS BORN IN CLAVERACK

Margaret Sanger was another of Claverack College's most well-known students. She holds the distinction of having introduced the controversial idea of birth control, a virtual ban on babies, which would eventually make her one of the most well-regarded women in American history.

While at Claverack, she was Maggie Higgins. In 1895, she enrolled with the hopes of entering medical school in the future. Though her family did not have the means to pay tuition to a private and prestigious boarding school, her parents and sisters scraped together the funds. She was among more than three hundred students attending the institution, and the campus was massive, including several buildings over twenty acres accommodating students with classrooms, housing, a gymnasium, armory and more. The class selection was equally extensive, and Maggie Higgins first gravitated toward standard courses like penmanship and accounting. She then moved on to literary pursuits. In Higgins's time at Claverack, the school was already on the decline, feeling the economic pressure from running such an elaborate institution and the competition from other educational options; four years after she left, the college closed.

The experience at Claverack must have changed Higgins because she entered as Maggie and left using the name Margaret. Yet she continued at the school as a working student, holding down menial jobs waiting tables and depending on scholarships to fund her education. She became a confident student and drew criticism for her outspokenness on women's rights and equality for women in her writings. Despite her working-class upbringing, she learned gentrification from her fellow students and attracted both men and women. She tended to break the rules, leaving the school for parties in Hudson and unauthorized outings. By 1897, her family funds had run out, forcing her to leave Claverack College. She briefly took a job as a teacher before returning to her hometown of Corning, New York, to nurse her dying mother. She eventually gravitated toward nursing, and in 1902 she married Bill Sanger, a Jewish immigrant who was still living with his parents at age twenty-six. She became pregnant six months into the marriage, and she also became ill with tuberculosis, which she had had earlier and probably contracted from her mother. She spent long periods of time in a sanitarium in the Catskills to get well. Upon her return home, she devoted herself to domestic life, which she would come to detest.

As a nurse she assisted in delivering babies and experienced the plight of poor women who had jeopardized their health for pregnancies. Sanger joined New York's Socialist Party. She believed in freethinkers. She lectured on health issues to educate women about their own bodies. Her fight for birth control started when she published a small magazine called

The Woman Rebel, and the federal government indicted her for using the mail to distribute obscene material to advocate birth control. She opened her first birth control clinic in 1916 and was arrested. In 1921, Sanger founded the American Birth Control League, which later became the Planned Parenthood Federation of America.

Dam the Downpour

The only village in the town of Claverack is called Philmont. In 1938, Philmont took the full force of one of the strongest and most serious storms ever to hit the Northeast and New England. This was a time before talk of global warming, before twenty-four-hour news channels and national weather service alerts on cellphones. The storm came in over the Atlantic, along New York's coastline, without much time for warning. Instead of staying steadily to the east, it pushed hard west with winds exceeding 186 miles per hour. The damaging winds were a threat, but it was the way that the wind swept the water up into thick storm clouds and positioned them inland that produced the worst destruction ever seen in the little village. Early settlers in Philmont were drawn to the unique hill town because of the excellent waterways weaving through the landscape. They used the streams and waterfalls to power manufacturing mills and crafted a dam to create a reservoir in the village center. In spite of this good planning, Philmont suffered severely. The rain clouds moved in and dropped a deluge of wild water. Small streams bulged, creeks careened over their edges and ponds poured out. The overflow blocked streets, stranded residents and railroad passengers and killed phone lines.

On the day of the storm, September 21, the waters filled the town's reservoir, causing the man-made dam to act like a steamroller through the village. The force was so strong it uprooted trees, tore up pavement, plucked out telephone poles and demolished everything in its path. Huge waves careened down Ark Street dragging down with it Ames Street and a few others boulevards. The entire mess slogged through the neighboring hamlet of Melenville, where the debris and water gouged out the earth, creating a massive ravine at Route 217. The day after, citizens of Philmont realized the damage. Whole front lawns were literally peeled away like the skin of an apple, and houses were swept off their foundations. With evacuations and luck, miraculously no one was harmed.

CLAVERACK

Scene of Philmont. *From* The History of Columbia County, *author's collection*.

Before the hurricane of 1938 ended, it took over six hundred lives and caused over $300 million in damage throughout Connecticut, Rhode Island, Massachusetts and New York. Philmont sustained over $100,000 worth of damage, and Columbia County as a whole lost over $1 million in property.

Ollie-Wood

In addition to its history of mills and a flood that almost wiped the village off the map, Philmont's hidden history tells the story of how it became known as "Olliewood." Few know that U.S. Marine Corps lieutenant Oliver "Ollie" North, who was at the center of the Iran-Contra political scandal, grew up in Philmont.

By all accounts, the North family members were model citizens of Philmont and Oliver L., generally known as Larry, was a likable guy, serving at the local church as an alter boy and as an honorable Boy Scout. In 1987, ABC news deployed a reporter on "special assignment" to Philmont to interview townspeople about Oliver North's character. Reporter Betsy Aaron found that everyone described Larry as polite and outgoing. His former coach offered a similar account. Though following the famous North trial, the opinion of North in Philmont changed dramatically.

Though "Olliemania" had settled down in Washington, the people of Philmont were still angry at North's disgrace. To show their displeasure, the village hosted the "Larry North Day" in August 1987, which included a parade down Main Street with two hundred protesters honoring their hometown hero. The *New York Times* reported on the event and wrote that more than one thousand spectators showed up for the event; however, Oliver North did not. Many of the stores in town sold popcorn, hot dogs and souvenirs and displayed large signs mocking North, which read "Welcome to Olliewood."

4
HUDSON

There is no history of Columbia County without an exploration of the early days of Hudson, New York.

LAND HO! HAIL HUDSON

Henry Hudson was probably the first European explorer to visit the site of what is now the city of Hudson sailing off the shores in his ship, the *Half Moon*, in 1609. Whether he first touched ground in Hudson, Stockport or Castleton is a scholarly discussion that will continue far into the future. Looking back, it is safe to say that Hudson wove his way around the small islands directly across from the current docks of downtown Hudson, and the city was named for the Hudson River and, ultimately, the English explorer himself.

On any map, old or new, you can see that Hudson is not a big place, but it has big history. As with all of Columbia County, the land was first inhabited by Mohican Indians. The Dutch followed in the seventeenth century. One of them, Jan Franz Van Hoesen, purchased a large tract of land from the Indians in 1662. His farm included the area of Hudson plus part of what is now Greenport. The area was originally part of Claverack, called Claverack Landing, and served as a port for the surrounding areas. The original Claverack Landing contained only a few stores, wharves and a canoe ferry.

Hidden History of Columbia County, New York

Henry Hudson's Half Moon *1609 Being Met by the Mohicans. Courtesy of the Library of Congress.*

In 1783, a group of men who were experts on the sea and well versed in whaling came from Nantucket, Massachusetts, and Providence and Newport, Rhode Island, seeking a safe harbor for their ships because of attacks by the British navy. When they saw Claverack Landing with its high bluffs, deep waters and two bays, they instructed a group of their men to seek out and buy large tracts of land.

These men had wealth, and so they purchased much more extensive land than what is now Hudson. By the fall of that year, two families had joined them. In the spring of 1784, more families arrived. They brought with them portable houses that had been prefabricated in Nantucket and bore unique New England–styled architecture. By all accounts, these dwellings may very well have been the first manufactured homes ever created.

Small City Is Big News

This group of men called themselves the "Proprietors," and they included Thomas Jenkins, Gideon Gardner and David Laurence. They methodically continued to buy large quantities of real estate in and around Hudson including the home of Colonel Van Alen.

Hudson

Warren Street in 1890, Hudson, New York. *Collection of Jon and April Meredith, Kinderhook, New York.*

The group met regularly and laid out the streets and built brick and stone houses while improving the wharf and Hudson's harbor. Businesses thrived, and so did the port, which became the second largest in New York by 1784. In 1785, an act was passed to make Hudson a city. The rise of the small city became big news throughout the state and caused many people to move there seeking to be part of the exciting development. The *New York Journal* of 1786 talked of this "unparalleled increase with several wharves, one hundred and fifty houses, shops, barns and one of the best distilleries in America."

The city had its first fire in 1793, when the office of the *Hudson Gazette* and the bookstore of Ashbel Stoddard both burned. With no equipment or men to extinguish the fire, the town Proprietors took up a petition to create organized fire companies. The official ordinance required houses with fireplaces of two or more to have leather buckets with the owners' initials on them and at least two gallons of water. These buckets were required to be filled and hung near the front door of each home. Anyone violating the ordinance was fined six shillings. Soon after, a fire engine was ordered and firemen put in place. The wells in town were made accessible to the firemen. Night watchmen were hired who were later developed into the city's first police department. Public lights came on in 1798, though primitive, and often the lights were lit only when the moon was not lighting the sky.

Fireman's Convention, Hudson, New York, turn of the century. *Courtesy of Jon and April Meredith, Kinderhook, New York.*

The destruction of Ashbel Stoddard's property was a major loss for Hudson. Stoddard was one of the city's first settlers originating from Saybrook, Connecticut. He was a staunch Congregationalist and then became more liberal. His establishment consisted of a printing office, a bookstore and a bindery. On April 7, 1785, he released the first issue of the

Hudson Weekly Gazette. The job of printing in this time period took tremendous work. The type on pages was set by hand. Delivery was even more precarious with the publisher paying post riders to deliver the news to paid subscribers who could live a huge distance from the printer in undeveloped areas. In 1829, after fighting off stiff competition from other papers, Ashbel Stoddard closed the doors and ceased publishing the *Hudson Gazette*. Yet the people of Hudson had other ideas in mind. Raising $500, several of the citizens brought the paper back to life by purchasing Stoddard's equipment and type. In order to ensure the paper's longevity, they hired an intelligent young lawyer by the name of John Worth Edmonds and paid him the hefty sum of $3 a week to run the paper. Edmonds was on the rise with a budding legal career. He remained as editor for just two years but built a solid foundation. Stoddard had been immortalized in the year of 1812, when artist Ammi Phillips came to Hudson and painted portraits of Ashbel and his wife, Patience Bolles Stoddard.

Though there were many strong men with great characters in Hudson, Thomas Jenkins was the true leader of the Proprietors and was always consulted during difficult or important matters. When he died in 1808, the Proprietors' meetings dwindled. Yet without the hard work and perseverance of these men who had clearly laid the foundation for the city, Hudson would not have prospered. It's also not a surprise that these clever and intelligent businessmen were mostly Quakers who dedicated themselves to their liberal points of view.

Around the close of the War of 1812, Hudson began to decline. Businesses closed and the losses were heavily felt. When the Bank of Hudson closed in 1829, the city began a gradual depression. People left, and boats did too. The need for commerce resulted in a revival of the whaling companies that had been a thriving trade earlier in the city. This upswing lasted around fifteen years. Other businesses of all kinds sprung up from tailors to grocers, along with hardware businesses and companies that bought "uncurrent and currency" from broken banks. Hubbel, Clark & Co. ran the steamboat called *Fairfield*, which made three round trips per week to New Amsterdam (New York City). This traffic on the river helped bolster many establishments.

Rags to Riches to Rags

In 1818 a massive stone structure was built on State Street and first used as the almshouse for the city of Hudson. It was law in 1778 that cities and

Hidden History of Columbia County, New York

Hudson Asylum/Orphanage. *Courtesy of the Hudson Library History Room.*

towns take care of the poor. Towns like Hudson and Ghent prepared and maintained poorhouses. Prior to that, the poor were the responsibility of individual families.

The word *alms* is from Old English and means "pity or merciful" and can be traced back to early Christian and Buddhist religions. The first recorded almshouse was founded in York by King Athelstan; the oldest still in existence is the Hospital of St. Cross in Winchester, dating to about 1132. In the Middle Ages, the majority of European hospitals functioned as almshouses.

When the city relocated the residents of its almshouse to a poor farm farther out of town, the building was taken over by Dr. Samuel White for the establishment of an insane asylum under his own private auspices and supervision, assisted by Dr. G.H. White. "In the first ten years it was open, three hundred patients were admitted, most of whom were cured, and all were benefitted," notes an advertisement of the institution published in 1841. By their very nature, lunatic asylums are unsettling to the inhabitants, the caretakers and the towns in which they are located. Their very walls speak of pain and deep-seated suffering. While Columbia County was heralded for its spectacular scenery and healthful attributes, it also attracted its fair share of troubled souls.

Dr. White, however, had a very remarkable reputation. He was born in Connecticut on February 23, 1777. He began his professional career in

Hudson, New York, in 1797. Because the doctor had experienced insanity in his own family, he was led to study mental disorders. His reputation as a surgeon, as well as a general practitioner, and success as an alienist, made him known throughout the state. Interestingly enough "alien" in Hudson's history, and elsewhere, referred to mental illness, with alienism being "the study or treatment of mental diseases, especially in their relation to legal problems." Alienists were also referred to as "mad doctors." The term is derived from the French for "alienation" and the Latin origin *alienus*, or "belonging to another."

The asylum closed when the state mental hospital was opened in Utica. In 1851, the Hudson Female Academy was established in the building under the direction of Reverend J.B. Hague. The school enjoyed a "high reputation" and attracted students from as far away as Detroit, Milwaukee, the West Indies and Europe. Henry Ary, who painted the portrait of George Washington that was hung in the Common Council chamber in city hall, as well as numerous views of Mount Merino, the Hudson River and the city of Hudson, was on the faculty and taught drawing and painting to fourth-year students.

An 1853 catalogue of the academy offers this description of 400 State Street:

> *The building occupied by the Academy, was originally erected at a cost exceeding twelve thousand dollars. By an additional outlay it has been perfectly adapted to its present use. It is situated on a gentle eminence, commanding a view almost unrivaled in extent and magnificence. It contains a large and beautiful schoolroom, recitation rooms, and numerous other apartments, arranged for carrying on to the best advantage, the work of instruction. Hair Mattresses* [sic] *are used throughout sleeping apartments. Each room is carpeted, and furnished with table, bureau, &c., and in the arrangements generally regard has been had to comfort and elegance.*

In 1865, the Hudson Female Academy moved to a building at the corner of First and Warren Streets, and by 1878, when Ellis's *History of Columbia County* was published, it was no longer in existence.

When the Hudson Female Academy relocated, the building on State Street became the private residence of one of the school's trustees, George H. Power. George Power was a major force in the development of ferries and river transportation in Hudson. His father, Captain John Power, had come to Hudson from Adams, Massachusetts, in 1790 and began boating on the river as early as 1804 or 1805. He founded the freighting firm of Power, Livingston & Co. and owned the first steamboat in Hudson, the *Bolivar*.

George was born in Hudson in 1817 and began his career in the river at the age of seventeen as the master of a vessel owned by Jeremiah Bame. Eventually, George Power became the owner of the New York and Hudson Steamboat Company, the Hudson and Athens Ferry, and the Hudson and Catskill Ferry. The ferryboat that ran between Hudson and Athens bore his name. He was one of the original trustees of the Hudson City Savings Institution and served two terms as the mayor of Hudson. George H. Power lived at 400 State Street from 1865 until 1881, when he sold the building to the Hudson Orphan and Relief Association. Today, the building serves as a library and offers an extensive history room filled with rare books and a few artifacts.

Spirits, Sulpher Springs and Séances

Over the course of many years with the city's feverish growth and equally rapid decline, many people passed away in Hudson. Some perished and departed, and some apparently stayed on.

In *Haunted Places: The National Directory of Ghostly Abodes, Sacred Sites* by Dennis Hauk, the author clearly states that the Dietz House, built in the 1830s in Hudson, is haunted by Mabel Parker a woman who moved into the house in the early 1900s and lived there for nearly fifty years. Her family, who continued to occupy the house, reported that Mabel would walk the stairs and seize the covers off those who slept in the second-floor bedroom, the same room she had occupied in life.

Not far from Hudson is Stockport. It is, by far, the smallest of the eighteen towns in Columbia County. It was established from land from the towns of Stuyvesant, Ghent and Hudson on April 30, 1833. It received its name from Stockport, England, the native place of James Wild, a prominent resident of the town. To the west, it borders the Hudson River. Where the Stockport creek meets the Hudson, vineyards grew wildly, producing hundreds of tons of grapes. Some believe is here that Henry Hudson first landed.

With many waterways reaching into this small town, it made for a powerful water system, from which the town prospered. Originally, the northern portion of the town was included in the Powell and Kinderhook patents and the grants made to Major Abram Staats in 1667 and at subsequent periods. Major Staats was a surgeon attached to the garrison at Albany in 1643 and was among the earliest of the immigrants from Holland to America. Nearby Stottville was named for Jonathan Stott, who was an intelligent weaver of

Hudson

Sulpher Springs Hotel and Resort, Stottsville in the city of Hudson, New York. *Collection of Jon and April Meredith.*

satinets in Hudson. He located here in 1828 and began the manufacturing of flannels in a small factory, which employed only two sets of thirty-six-inch cards and twelve looms. A short distance east of the village of Stottsville is the celebrated Columbia White Sulphur Springs.

The presence of these springs was noted as early as 1830, and some wonderful cures were reported as the result of using their waters. It wasn't until 1855 that Charles B. Nash purchased and opened a house for the accommodation of invalids at the springs. Many who had failed to find relief from medical aid were cured by the waters. The Columbia Springs House was created much like Columbia Hall, which offered water cures in New Lebanon.

A few yards down the road, not far from Stockport is the village of Columbiaville. It was there that the Smiths lived, in an old stone house. The Smiths were so influential in the early 1800s that many know this area as Smithville. In this house, a family member by the name of Aunt Rachel was among a group of Spiritualists who held séances.

The Spiritualist movement attested that the souls of the dead resided in an astral realm and could communicate with the living. Through traveling medium shows that exhibited spirit rappings, table tippings and thought readings, as well as published communiqués from famous dead people, the belief of Spiritualism spread quickly across America.

One of Hudson's most unusual residents in particular was responsible for putting Spiritualism on the map in America. John Worth Edmonds was born in Hudson in 1799. Spiritualists believed that they could communicate with the dead. In *The Spirit Book: The Encyclopedia of Clairvoyance, Channeling, and Spirit* by Raymond Buckland, the author says Edmonds "is the man who has done the most to make the movement of spiritualism the vital force and power that it has become." Around the time Edmonds turned eighteen in 1819, he studied law and entered Martin Van Buren's law practice in Albany. He succeeded in becoming part of both branches of the state legislature of New York, president of the senate and judge of the Supreme Court of New York. Edmonds was also noted for having overseen the trial of Big Thunder during the anti-rent wars. During a heated debate between the two lawyers presiding over Big Thunder's case, John Edmonds put John Van Buren (the second son of Martin Van Buren) and Ambrose L. Jordon in jail overnight to cool off.

Edmonds was, in every sense of the phrase, a straight and upstanding citizen, yet he became drawn to Spiritualism after a period of deep depression and contemplation following his wife's death, during which he questioned whether what he had heard from preachers was true and whether there was indeed a life after death.

Edmonds first tried to prove that the Spiritualist movement was fraudulent, but he then became a firsthand witness to mental and physical mediums. He became so convinced that what he was seeing was true that he kept 1,600 pages of meticulous records. When Judge Edmonds went public with his findings in a book in 1853, simply titled *Spiritualism*, he was attacked by the press,

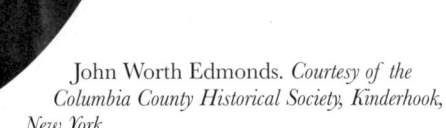

John Worth Edmonds. *Courtesy of the Columbia County Historical Society, Kinderhook, New York.*

the church and politicians and was forced to resign his post on the bench and return to private practice.

It was about that time that Edmonds developed his own abilities as a medium, and between the years 1853 and 1854, he and a group of friends received many communications. Among those coming through from the other side were Emanuel Swedenborg, the original founder of Spiritualism, and Roger Bacon, an English philosopher and early alchemist born around 1213 who is believed to have discovered gunpowder.

Edmonds's daughter, Laura, also developed powers that allowed her to speak in tongues. Though she was barely schooled in French, while in a trance she was able to speak Spanish, French, Greek, Italian, Portuguese, Latin, Hungarian and Indian languages.

Edmonds's best-known writings appeared in the two volumes of *Spiritualism*. His message in the book offered that the gift of knowledge of spiritual things is available to all. Spiritualism gave rise to a belief in spirit contact, which appealed to many celebrated people of the time. Elizabeth Barrett Browning, William Cullen Bryant, Thomas Carlyle, Emily Dickinson, Sir William Crookes, Edgar Allen Poe, Alfred Russell Wallace, Mark Twain, Harriet Beecher Stowe, Queen Victoria and W.B. Yeats were all investigators and proponents of the new spiritual science. The movement grew rapidly and became so popular that in 1926, an anti-fortunetelling bill was introduced in Washington. If passed, it would have outlawed the psychic arts for monetary gain, making it punishable by a fine and/or imprisonment. Harry Houdini even testified before a congressional subcommittee against the spiritualist mediums; however, because of the constitutional guarantee of religious freedom, the proposed ban failed to pass Congress.

Edmonds eventually died in 1874 from a long illness while in New York City. In notes he left about his own funeral, Edmonds wished to be interred in the same coffin as his dead wife. They are buried together in Hudson.

Sin City

When you bring up Hudson in casual conversation, people are often surprised to find out that as late as the 1950s it was known as Sin City.

It seems this trend started back in early days when the whaling trade in Hudson brought to town transient sailors who frequented houses of ill repute on Diamond Street (now Columbia Street). Perhaps prostitution began as an innovative cottage industry in Hudson, but at its peak in the 1920s and '30s, there were at least fifteen different establishments open for business that were serviced by over seventy-five professional women and girls.

In fact for about 160 years, prostitution was a fairly normal service utilized by locals and out-of-town visitors and was very much an intricate portion of the town's economy. It boosted the tourist trade and helped the town prosper.

People flocked to Hudson particularly to partake in these pleasures, and when they arrived, they needed places to eat, went to bars and bought gas (after the advent of automobiles), clothing, incidentals and so on. Naturally, if whorehouses were the mainstay of local commerce, one could imagine that gambling wasn't far away, and soon enough, illegal betting parlors operated openly as well. With everyone satisfied and making money, it seems that the industry went unnoticed and undisturbed for quite some time despite the evidence of illegal operations taking place. It is easy to visualize Hudson as perhaps a version of New Orleans's famous Bourbon Street during Mardi Gras with bordellos to the left and to the right.

The crackdown on prostitution finally occurred in Hudson in 1950, with the New York State Troopers raiding the brothels during a torrid sweep that was initiated by the Governor Tom Dewey. In 1951, the scales tipped even more when the New York State Crime Commission investigated allegations of crime and corruption of local officials. The damning accusations came from people within the trade, and many prominent men were named. Perhaps it was because law enforcement men looked the other way that the prostitutes of Hudson were able to continue to make a tidy business in this town and underworld gambling was able to live in the dim red glow of the Diamond District for so many years.

In present-day Hudson, life is bustling with economic growth and the hope of prosperity for the fresh and energetic pioneers who continue to flock to the resilient city that overlooks the great river. Yet with an ironic inability to completely shake off its past, Hudson has the dubious distinction as the home of some of New York State's most renowned prisons and facilities for reform.

5
KINDERHOOK

KIDS OF THE CREEK

In 1609, when Hendrick Hudson sailed up the river, it is likely that he anchored his ship near Kinderhook. The word *kinderhook* was used when Hudson sat anchored in the great river. From a distance, he saw the Mohican Indian families grouped on the shore. It was then he applied the Dutch word for "children's corner" or *kinderhoeck*.

In his own journal, Hudson wrote, "I sailed to the shore in one of their canoes with an old man, who was the chief of the tribe consisting of forty men and seventeen women; these I saw there in a house well constructed of oak-bark and circular in shape, so that it had the appearance of being built with an arched roof."

The Mohicans, who Hudson met in what is now Columbia County, were from the Lenni-Lenapes, which means "original people." These Indians were descendants of the Algonquian-language tribe who once controlled a considerable portion of the area. In order for the Dutch settlers to make this new land their home, they would need to negotiate land sales with the Mohicans. Yet this is where cultural differences turned to grave misunderstandings, and ultimately, these misinterpretations changed the course of destiny for the native Mohican tribe forever.

The hidden history in Kinderhook and throughout the county really starts with the Mohicans. One little-known fact is that Mohicans and Native Americans in general didn't believe in land ownership. For them, there was

The Arrival of Hendrick Hudson. Courtesy of the Library of Congress.

simply tribal territory. Most Indians also believed that everything had a spirit. Europeans, on the other hand, believed that nature could and should be tamed and improved by human effort (based on the verse in Genesis to "Lord over the earth"). Thus, when the Europeans came to trade for land, the Native Americans didn't understand their concept of outright ownership. They thought it only meant to share. William Cronan summed up their mentality in *Changes in the Land*: "Only the land lives forever. How can a human being 'own' land?"

The Mohicans were a loving people who lived close to the river known to them as the Mahicannituck. They were friendly, self-sufficient and cherished the earth. Yet as more European settlers came, the Mohicans lost access to their land and their ability to find food; therefore, they made fewer tools of their own and depended more and more on what the white men could provide. Worse yet, they were dying from smallpox, measles and diphtheria and lost whole villages to diseases. Eventually, they were pushed farther north and east by aggressive Mohawk tribes. The Dutch made peace with the Mohicans in order to create a fur trade according to the Norman's Kill peace treaty of

Kinderhook

Historic New York State Mohicans sign on the Taconic Parkway. *Courtesy of Stephen Kent Comer.*

Kinderhook Square in the mid-1800s. *Collection of Jon and April Meredith, Kinderhook, New York.*

1617. As a result of this peace, the Mohicans were further subjugated. When their humiliation became intolerable, the Mohicans revolted.

The Indian war over land and trade lingered for three long years until 1628. Unable to escape an ambush on Roger's Island (now known as Green Island), the Mohicans admitted defeat. The Mohicans, popularized by the famous story *The Last of the Mohicans* by James Fennimore Cooper, retreated. The remaining tribe members moved toward Taghkanic and eventually Stockbridge, Massachusetts.

In essence, Kinderhook is a result of a land transaction between the settlers and the Mohicans. In 1686, the royal governor granted the Great Kinderhook Patent, which reaffirmed prior patents and organized these tracts into one township.

Among the parcels covered by the patent was the present site of the village, which had originally been conveyed by the Mohican chief Emikee. According to the deed of record, a resident of the manor of Rensellaerswyck, Martin Cornelisse van Buren (1638–1703), was one of the original thirty-one patentees and was President Martin Van Buren's great-great-grandfather.

Curious Case of Martin Van Buren

Today, Kinderhook is well known as the home of Martin Van Buren, the country's eighth president. Van Buren's first wife, Hannah, was somewhat of a mystery. Hannah Hoes Van Buren was born in Kinderhook on March 8, 1783, to Johannes Dirksen Hoes and Maria Quackenbush, also of Kinderhook. Through her mother, Hannah was a relative of Theodore Roosevelt. Through both their maternal and paternal lines, Hannah and Martin Van Buren were closely related, and it was rumored they were first cousins, once removed.

It was reported that Hannah and Martin were childhood sweethearts, but no one knows for certain why they waited until after Martin was twenty-four years old and had been trained as a lawyer to marry. In their first year of marriage, they moved to Hudson, where Martin became heavily involved in politics. Together they had five sons, of whom only four survived, and a daughter who was stillborn. Hannah Van Buren devoted herself to being a great hostess. In fact, along with her own family, the Van Burens also lived with Martin's law partners. She became involved in the charitable work of the local Presbyterian Church, which she joined in Albany. Sadly, it was

One of only two portraits of Hannah Van Buren. *Courtesy of the Martin Van Buren Historic Site, Kinderhook, New York.*

there she contracted tuberculosis. Though she was so ill she was unable to get out of bed for more than short periods of time, she became pregnant in that time period. While she and her child survived for a time, the birth weakened her tremendously.

She died soon after giving birth in 1817. Though her husband claimed that she had been a driving force in his early life, her name is omitted from his lengthy eight-hundred-page autobiography. Some reports say he never mentioned his wife to his children as they grew older, to the point that his second son was unsure of his mother's first name. Perhaps unable to rid himself of his grief, Van Buren remained a widower for eighteen years and was single when he entered the White House. Van Buren's history continued in the realm of strangeness followed by more bad luck.

Within several months of taking office in 1837, an economic crisis known as the panic of 1837 erupted when nine hundred banks collapsed, leading to an economic depression that lasted throughout Van Buren's presidency. His political enemies would come to refer to him as Martin Van Ruin, blaming him not only for the economic depression in the first place but also for his failure to resolve it despite the fact that he established the federal treasury to protect government funds.

There is a curious pattern related to Martin Van Buren that borders on the occult as it relates to numbers. Van Buren served under Andrew Jackson as the eighth vice president of the United States. Later, he became the eighth president of the United States. After his presidency, he lived to see the election of eight more presidents, each from eight different states. He was also the first in a consecutive string of eight one-term presidents. Earlier in his career, he had been the eighth elected governor of New York. In the preceding paragraphs and in the ones that follow, notice how many times "eight" is included.

Van Buren had a love of riding horses, and he loved other animals, too. In fact, when he received a gift of two tiger cubs from the sultan of Oman, he had every intention of raising them, yet by law, he wasn't allowed to keep the gifts and was forced to return the tigers. Van Buren also spoke fluent Dutch and was the very first American-born citizen to take the White House.

Though unsubstantiated, it was rumored that Van Buren was the illegitimate son of Aaron Burr. This idea most likely grew out of fact that while growing up in Kinderhook, Van Buren's father owned a tavern in town where Burr and Alexander Hamilton where frequent guests.

As is the case for many well-known luminaries, Martin Van Buren never attended college. A lawyer with a firm in Albany who owed his father a favor and brought the young Martin Van Buren in as a law clerk where he swept floors and learned the law at night.

The abbreviation "OK" has many stories related to Martin Van Buren. It first related to "Old Kinderhook," where Van Buren was born and later where he retired. Van Buren was also known as "Old Kinderhook." Yet one tidbit explains that he would leave notes to his secretary when going away for the weekend that read, "Off to Kinderhook" and later would simply read, "OK."

And there are more hidden facts about Kinderhook's most noted resident. The famous author Washington Irving and Martin Van Buren were close friends. Washington Irving visited Kinderhook many times, first as a tutor

KINDERHOOK

Martin Van Buren postcard. *Collection of Jon and April Meredith, Kinderhook, New York.*

Washington Irving, portrait. *Courtesy of the Library of Congress.*

to the Peter Van Ness family, original owners of the Lindenwald Estate. The home was previously owned by the Van Ness family and was where Washington Irving wrote most of his book A History of New York.

One of Peter Van Ness's sons was William P. Van Ness, whose main claim to fame is that as Aaron Burr's personal friend, he communicated Burr's challenge to Alexander Hamilton and acted as his second at the fateful duel. According to local legend, Van Ness gave Burr refuge in a secret sealed room at Lindenwald after he killed Hamilton.

Van Buren and Irving met in London, in New York and in Hoboken, New Jersey, where they visited several old Dutch communities. They frequently wrote letters to each other. During his stay in Kinderhook, Irving wrote "Rip Van Winkle" and began his famous story "The Legend of Sleepy Hollow." One letter written by Washington Irving attests to the fact that Ichabod Crane was patterned after Jesse Merwin, who taught at Kinderhook's local schoolhouse, and that many of the other characters were based on people he met in the village.

There's also a lovely story about how Martin Van Buren became muddied in a pothole when visiting the Quaker village of Friendly Folk in Indiana. Van Buren's stagecoach mysteriously tipped over, and he found himself face down in the dirt. According to the story in *Indiana: A Guide to the Hoosier State*, Van Buren was passing through in 1840 on a campaign swing and had previously vetoed a bill there for improvement of the roads. Clearly the citizens had something to say about the need for better roads.

Tracks and Traces

During the Revolutionary War, the Kinderhook area was the site of several historic events. In the winter of 1775–76, Colonel Henry Knox transported a critical cache of artillery from the recently captured Fort Ticonderoga to the desperate city of Boston. Using ox and horse-drawn sledges, Knox led his troops through impossible conditions, frozen land and deep woods, rarely stopping to rest and infrequently replenishing their meager food and water caches. The Knox path weaves unevenly through Columbia County, though one of path's sections is situated directly in the town of Kinderhook.

Knox was reportedly a giant at over six feet tall and 250 pounds. He came up with a brilliant solution to transport a cannon from Fort Ticonderoga by moving it over three hundred miles during the winter to arrive in Boston by the spring of 1776. Washington, who was at a stalemate in Boston, approved the mission. With his brother, Henry, Knox traveled over frozen roads, where they found not only the canon but also eighteen pieces of artillery, including guns, howitzers and muskets and the amunition to go along with them. The odds were stacked against him, yet he moved the weighted transport with forty-two sleds and eighty oxen. He traveled through Albany and then waited until the Hudson River was frozen to a safe thickness to cross. Despite careful planning, one cannon was lost through a break in the ice. They made it to the Old Post Road in Kinderhook before being met by heavy snow. At Claverack, the exhausted party spent the night at the Dutch Reformed Church and then was delayed again with a sled that had broken down. They made it to the Berkshire foothills into Massachusetts. The group arrived in Boston to aid Washington in his fight on March 2, 1776. In Kinderhook there are markers commemorating the roles that it and Columbia County played in the transport of the big guns.

DOWNTON ABBEY OF KINDERHOOK

Van Buren was a man who believed in equality, but he also believed in having domestic help serve him in his home at Lindenwald. Because he was a widower with several sons living at home, he employed a battalion of Irish Catholic women as servants to keep his house in order. Both older women and younger girls were on call twenty-four hours a day and summoned through an intricate system of call bells wired in and out of the walls at the Van Buren estate, which is now a National Historical Site.

Famine in Ireland propelled the rise in Irish immigrants to Columbia County and its surroundings in the mid-1800s, around the time Van Buren's political career ended and he retired for good to Kinderhook at Lindenwald. After a thorough and stylish renovation of the home, Van Buren filled his house with fine furniture and then, soon thereafter, came a continuous stream of friends, visitors and overnight guests. With a large family in residence and so many lavish parties going on, the servants were busy all the time.

The domestic staff entered the house through a door in the basement, where the kitchen was stationed and where they spent most of their day. They slept under the eaves in the attic in tight-fitting rooms outfitted with compact bells above the doors that were operated with a simple pull or a tug from the

The servant call bell installed in the upper wing of the old servant's quarters at Lindenwald, home of Martin Van Buren. *Taken by the author with permission from the Martin Van Buren Historic Site, Kinderhook, New York.*

master of the house. The servants experienced a physical distance from the family that underscored their social distance. On the far side of the home, hidden away is an amazing spiral staircase that spans the full height of the house. It was used exclusively by the help and required servants to climb up eighty-eight narrow, twisting steps with trays, food, heavy laundry baskets and the like in their arms as they traveled from the basement to other locations in the house.

The call bell system was rather silent, yet with just a pulley and wire system it created a subtle communication between Van Buren and his staff that didn't require much effort and needed no speaking at all. Remarkably one of the original bells in the system has survived at Lindenwald, and the full system has now been properly restored. Some local folklore implies that Van Buren's former cook, Aunt Sarah, who was the only servant to sleep in the basement, still watches over the kitchen though she has long passed on; however, there are no verifiable reports that tell us whether the servant's call bell has ever been heard ringing.

Near Kinderhook's village is the slave cemetery. The headstones are tipped, turned and twisted by the continual movement of frost under frozen earth, which has displaced them year after year since the early eighteenth century when the town census defined 293 of its residents as slaves. By 1780, that number had grown to 638, more slaves than in the towns of Claverack and Hudson combined. These servants were owned predominately by families with large farms until slavery was abolished in 1827. The words "loving and loyal" are in paragraphs written about the slaves of Kinderhook, and benevolent behavior was shown by masters of the time; yet on the gravestones, barely visible, was simply one name. When slaves were freed, they often adopted the name of the men who bound them, such as Van Buren, Van Ness and Vanderpoel.

6
New Lebanon

Taking the Waters

The historian Bancroft once said, "New Lebanon is the most beautiful valley on the top of the earth."

Fifteen miles from Kinderhook there once was the Mohican village of Kaunameek, now called New Lebanon. It is a place that today seems like a forgotten highway with unadorned houses, a modest diner, a firehouse and an Off Track betting parlor. Yet New Lebanon is deeply imbedded in the country's medical history, and it is rich with stories of mysticism and miracles.

It is thought that the original village lay close to the hamlet of Brainard (near Rayville) bordering Rensselaer County. It is there, somewhere on the banks of the Kinderhook Creek, that you can find the remains of an old Mohican burying ground.

Six miles away, in the center of the town of New Lebanon is the Indian Blessings Fountain monument located next to the town hall made by the world-famous sculptor Henry Hudson Kitson, who was born in England but lived in Tyringham, Massachusetts.

The fountain is dedicated to the Mohicans, who taught the early settlers about the healing powers of the unique spring that still flows down Mount Lebanon and through the town. There is something poetic about this in that the Mohicans where known as the "people of the waters that are never still."

The word *healing* weaves its way through New Lebanon's history like stray vines climbing in and out of frail saplings in the woods. The story of

Indian Blessings Fountain, Lebanon Springs, New York. The statue was created by Henry Hudson Kitson, sculptor, of Tyringham, Massachusetts. *Collection of Jon and April Meredith, Kinderhook, New York.*

New Lebanon

New Lebanon includes the hope of miracle cures, miraculous crafts and miraculous devotion to God.

At the base of the mountain in New Lebanon is a section of town known as Lebanon Springs. The Mohicans called the thermal springs they found

Lebanon Healing Springs original deed signed by "Goodrich." *Courtesy of Lebanon Valley Historical Society, New Lebanon, New York.*

there *Montepoale*, or "mountain pool." The area was also known originally as Willow Spring for the large willow that casts a shadow over the healing mountain waters where the Indians bathed. The tree, more likely a sycamore, still stands next to the updated pump house near historic ruins.

Captain Hitchcock, a captain in the British army, visited this place in 1756. There he found the spring in a small clearing, carefully framed with logs backed with clay. Some say that the Indians led the ailing Hitchcock to the warm springs. Hitchcock suffered from skin infections, and the springs healed him. He made Lebanon Springs his home in 1771, becoming one the first settlers and the first white man to inhabit this spot.

The land was originally owned by Captain Charles Goodrich, who obtained a land grant—the "Keyes grant"—of six thousand acres in Pittsfield, Massachusetts, in 1761, of which New Lebanon was a part. He leased the land where the thermal spring ran to Hitchcock in 1778 with a provision that the springs' miraculous healing waters be used for the public good.

Hitchcock constructed a house with a small bathroom attached and took a fee from visitors to use the bath. It wasn't long before the spring's popularity grew with added larger bathhouses, large tubs and luxury accommodations, where guests could enjoy the waters, which maintained an even temperature of seventy-three degrees Fahrenheit year-round. The water's medicinal properties were true. With testimonials for their use in treating "eczema, flesh-poisoning, scald-heads, arthritis, cutaneous diseases generally, morbid conditions of the liver, constipation, dyspepsia, chronic and inflammatory rheumatism, bronchitis, diseases of the kidneys, grout, and nervous diseases generally" from certified physicians, there seemed no end to the amazing abilities of this water. The springs continually offered a remarkable five hundred gallons of water per minute and still do today.

Hotels were erected one after another, including the great Columbia Hall in 1794, which accommodated three hundred people. Its surrounding thirty-eight acres allowed guests to breath fresh air on country walks. It was easily the most renowned resort in the state. With the help of the Boston and Albany Railroad lines at Canaan Four Corners and Pittsfield, it drew huge summer crowds looking for relief from a number of ailments. In the early 1800s, the Marquis De Lafayette and his son visited Columbia Hall. They brought with them as escorts General Solomon Van Rensselaer, Colonel Clinton, Colonel Cooper, Major Van Schaack and other officers of Colonel Cooper's regiment. The Hall has also been visited by many other celebrities and, in early times, was a favorite resort of the Livingstons and other old families of the state. Other notables who signed the guest list at

New Lebanon

Original Lebanon Springs Hotel, Columbia Hall. *Courtesy of Lebanon Valley Historical Society.*

the Columbia Hotel included Henry Longfellow, Charles Dickens, Daniel Webster and John Quincy Adams.

One of the most important places that sprung up in New Lebanon Springs was the Water Cure Establishment, opened in May of 1845 under the management of New Lebanon resident Joel Shew, who was a co-owner and an advising physician. This is where the first U.S. hydropathic facility was born and launched hydrotherapy curative treatment. "Water Curists" believed that illness was caused by the body being in unnatural states. Shew and his colleagues explained that by continually washing the body internally and externally, sometimes even wrapping the body in wet sheets, one could cleanse the body of lethal toxins. In essence, Shew, along with Priessnitz and others, created an entirely new health reform.

The treatment center that Shew constructed cost about $3,000. Its manager for ten years was Dr. David Campbell, also a New Lebanon resident. The elaborate cure center required the building of a mile-long aqueduct to access the precious healing waters of the mountain. Baths were built in various shapes and sizes to accommodate and cleanse every part of the ailing body. When Shrew left Lebanon to return to his medical practice in New York City, Dr. Norman Bedortha took on the water cure establishment. Those running the establishment claimed that it could cure what was incurable, and over two hundred testimonials were recorded and documented by the lucky patients who benefitted from the waters. Dr. Shew went on to create establishments in other parts of New York, and he published the *New York Water Cure Journal*, which had "attained an extent of circulation equalled [sic] by few monthlies in the world." The magazine's tag line was simple, "Wash and Be Healed."

Joel's wife, Marie Louise Shew, wrote a book about women's care that her husband edited. It was called the *Water-cure for Ladies: a Popular Work on the Health, Diet, and Regimen of Females and Children, and the Prevention and Cure of Diseases; with a Full Account of the Processes of Water-Cure*.

Shew and his wife of New Lebanon had roles to play in the beginnings of vegetarianism. Water curists like Shew believed in meat abstention, arguing that vegetables had far more nutrients than meat and were the overall answer to optimal health. Combining articles about water cures and a meatless diet, Shew's journal subscription grew to twenty-five thousand in 1850. A dietary reform movement exploded, and the American Vegetarian Society was born. Many followed Shew's lead, and "Meat Abstainers" from around the country gathered in New York City on May 15, 1850, for their first convention. The convention concluded agreeing that a vegetarian diet was the most natural and spiritually perfect one for humans.

Female Incarnation of Christ

Many healing mysteries intermingled in New Lebanon's hidden history. One religious group fled to the American colonies in 1774 to escape persecution in England and established a utopian society at Mount Lebanon. The group became known as the Shakers and was led by Ann Lee.

Ann Lee was born in 1736 into wretched conditions in Manchester, England. As a poor child, she was sent to work rather than attending school. Though illiterate, she understood industry from working in a cotton factory cutting velvet. Personal tragedies in her life brought Ann to believe that relations between a man and a woman were sinful. So convinced of this truth, she even attempted to stop sex between her parents. Despite this strong belief, she submitted to pressure from her parents and agreed to a marriage with Abraham Stanley, a blacksmith. Lee was desperately unhappy in England.

New Lebanon

She was unhappy in her arranged marriage and suffered emotionally from the death of all four of her infant children.

In 1758, at age twenty-one, she met James and Jane Wardley and joined the Wardley Society, a religious group that had broken away from the Quakers. Because the Wardleys' version of religious worship included shakings of the body and motions of the head and arms, they became known as "Shaking Quakers." The Shakers believed in open confession and the power of God against evil. Ann found protection and knowledge there and took to praying and fasting. During this time, she received a vision from God in which "the whole spiritual world seemed displayed before her."

This vision strengthened her beliefs, and she preached powerfully. Her sermons soon became so threatening to nonbelievers that she was often put in prison. To escape this abuse, Mother Ann, as she was known, left for America from Liverpool in May 1774 with a small group of followers, including her husband and brother. Despite a near shipwreck, they arrived in New York in August. The group took what lodging it could find, and Ann lived an austere life, offering to wash clothes to earn her keep. In that time, she nursed her ailing husband, Abraham. After he recovered, he rejected his wife's gospel, causing them to split permanently. When Ann sought to escape the city, one in her group, John Hocknell, went up the river and purchased a house at Niskayuna (now Watervliet) near Albany. Though Ann suffered tremendously during this time, she was rewarded with other visions that lifted her spirits. She and her followers believed Ann to be the second coming of Christ.

Once upstate, she was known to bring her small family group into the woods, where they would dance and sing. She began to shake during her sermons and speeches. The group's official name, which it used after immigrating to New York, was the "United Society of Believers in the Second Coming of Christ." In its earlier years, the group usually referred to itself as "Believers."

In 1780, Mother Ann's gospel was spreading beyond Niskayuna and drew people from other places, particularly New Lebanon, New York. It is during those meetings that the followers were so moved by the spirit they would quake, tremble, shake and speak in unknown tongues. The followers wished to attain freedom from sin the way Mother Ann and her elders had. Couples were told to reject the flesh. Men of faith came from New Lebanon to visit Mother Ann and confess to her. She then preached on the road in Enfield, Connecticut, and Harvard, Massachusetts, where she and her followers were consistently harassed and beaten by angry mobs. Taking refuge,

North family Shakers, New Lebanon, New York. *Collection of Jon and April Meredith, Kinderhook, New York.*

they visited the home of Israel Talcot on the mountain between New Lebanon and Hancock, Massachusetts, where Mother Ann took a dinner intended for four and spread it out among forty. She went on to John Bishop's house, and it was there they held their first meeting with over four hundred people in attendance. Eleazer Grant and Elisha Gilberts, Esquires, visited Mother Ann, as did a group of Indians who welcomed her. Her mission ultimately succeeded in America, where she traveled with her followers settling in New Lebanon.

Lee was against slavery and war. She fostered beliefs in neatness, economy, charity to the poor, celibacy and equality regardless of sex, race or temporal possessions. In her life, Mother Ann Lee reportedly cured the sick and performed miracles of healing of body and soul. She taught her followers to be industrious and put their hands to work and their hearts to God.

Hidden in the Shaker's history are remarkable inventions, for which they held exclusive patents. The washing machine, originally called the "wash mill," was developed by Nicholas Bennet of New Lebanon, and a patent for the washing machine was issued in January 1829 to a Shaker of Watervliet. Philemon Steward was issued a patent for the cast-iron fence post, and William J. Potter created a green corn–cutting machine. The common clothespin was a Shaker invention. With amazing creativity, the Shakers turned common brooms, buckets, tubs and pails into art forms.

New Lebanon

They made textiles and cloaks far superior to anything being produced at the time. In fact, it's believed that the Shakers at New Lebanon introduced "curved tailoring rules," allowing clothing to conform to the shape of the body. From 1789 to 1942, the Shakers made phenomenal chairs. In New Lebanon, there was a famous chair factory that made two dozen chairs a day in the latter part of 1872. From February 1884 to March 1885, records show that the Shakers shipped upward of three thousand chairs nationwide. The workmanship and elegance of these chairs were considered good enough to accommodate the divine. And of course, the Shakers were responsible for making baskets that are among the most beautiful ever recorded. The masterfulness of these pieces was perfected by complete devotion to the craft. They wove sewing baskets and bonnets and crafted dolls with clothes. They made chamois eyeglass cleaners, horsehair bushes, padded crutches and ingenious four-legged canes.

The Shakers were focused on living naturally and healthfully and believed in a clean and orderly life. They also followed an idea that "disease is an offense to God, and that it is in the power of men to be healthful, if they will."

There is evidence that the Mohicans understood the healing properties of the waters that ran along the Shaker dwellings of New Lebanon that fed a multitude of plants that grew close by. As was their way, the Indians shared their knowledge and their land with the community of neighbors in the valley, including the Shakers.

Mount Lebanon was eventually considered the "Holy Mount" and became the largest group of "Believers" communities with six hundred people, one hundred buildings and six thousand acres. Industrious and with sharpened business minds, Shakers filled a gap in the early 1800s when physicians had little or no knowledge of disease and common ailments and how to aid their patients who could easily die from a common cold. They produced herbs and supplied them to doctors, never prescribing them or selling them directly to individuals.

Some say that Shaker medicinals mirrored their social morals. In all, the Shakers gathered and grew more than four hundred herbs for medicine. The hundreds of thousands of tons of herbs they sold wholesale far exceeded their renowned furniture business. To keep up with demand, Shakers at Mount Lebanon built a huge herb house, where they could process and package fresh herbs efficiently and in quantities that would boggle the mind today.

Hidden History of Columbia County, New York

Tinctures from the Tildens

Tilden Pharmaceuticals advertisement. *Courtesy of Lebanon Valley Historical Society, New Lebanon, New York.*

Elam Tilden of New Lebanon watched with great interest how the Shaker herb phenomena and techniques were progressing in his town. In essence, he saw their success and wanted to profit from what they had uncovered. Tilden & Company planted forty of its own acres with medicinal herbs in the valley, and Tilden's work was noted in the *American Journal of Pharmacy* of 1881.

The Tildens had a long and equally fascinating history in New Lebanon. Elam Tilden was born in Lebanon, Connecticut, in 1781 to John Tilden and Bathsheba Janes. In 1824, Elam Tilden started growing, processing and selling herbal pharmaceuticals in New Lebanon. He established Tilden & Company, recognized as the oldest pharmaceutical company in the United States. For over 120 years, the agriculture and manufacturing of medicines changed New Lebanon. Elam was considered quite intelligent and clever, as his business expanded quickly with the help of his brother, Henry A. Tilden. The Tildens' developing pharmaceutical company was considered the "preeminent botanical house." Like the Shakers, the Tildens didn't prescribe cures but sold their herbs directly to physicians and published a booklet of formulas with instructions for using their products. Tilden passed the now world-renowned company

New Lebanon

to his sons, Moses Y. and Henry A. Tilden, who increased production. After their deaths, the company was incorporated in 1893 with Samuel Tilden as president with company offices in New York City and a branch in St. Louis. Samuel Jones Tilden was born in February 1841 to Elam Tilden and Polly Younglove. It was his grandfather John Tilden of Lebanon, Connecticut, who named the town of New Lebanon. Samuel went on to become a lawyer, the governor of New York and a one-time Democratic presidential candidate, running against Rutherford B. Hayes in 1876. In a close and very famous election, Tilden lost by one electoral vote despite winning the popular vote. He withstood this humiliation and, by many, was considered a rather extraordinary man. A copy of the *Phrenological Journal and Life Illustrated* described him: "This gentleman has a fine-grained organization, one that is very sensitive, susceptible to external and internal influences... He appreciates facts intuitively, and is more inclined to grasp truth by a direct, instinctive action of the mind, than to go through a plodding course of analysis. He forms his judgment first, and verifies the details afterward." Samuel Tilden is buried in a most handsome grave in the Cemetery of the Evergreens in New Lebanon.

Healing Hands

For a little place, New Lebanon has attracted a lot of attention. The spiritual movement of the Shakers and their healing herbs created an allure of sorts, summoning others who longed to uncover life's mysteries.

Lourdes is likely the place that is most well known for miracles. In a small village in France, thousands of devout Catholics make a pilgrimage each year to a tiny grotto, where there is a spring of healing water. For believers, it is on that exact spot in the year 1858 that the Virgin Mary revealed herself to a young girl, Bernadette Soubrious.

Some eighty-six years ago, in 1928, a priest by the name of John B. LeFebvro traveled to New Lebanon to be the pastor at the Church of the Immaculate Conception. Father LeFebvro had visited Lourdes. Upon descending into the New York valley of New Lebanon, he was overwhelmed by the same beauty he had experience at Lourdes and was inspired to create a shrine that is known today as "Our Lady of Lourdes Grotto."

During his time leading the church, it is reported that upward of one million people visited the shrine. It's an unusual structure, built like an

Immaculate Conception shrine St. Joseph's Parish, 1960, New Lebanon, New York. *From the author's collection.*

authentic cave with a massive opening made of natural stones and leading to hidden chambers. At its center is a statue of the Virgin as she appeared in the apparition at Lourdes. Strangely, the original church that sits alongside the grotto was situated at the base of Lebanon Mountain near the healing springs. The original church attracted parishioners from as far away as Pittsfield, Massachusetts, who traveled there on foot.

Today, New Lebanon looks forward. Though the Shakers have vanished and the healing spring hotels have closed, the Darrow School is still there, and the spiritual power of New Lebanon has not ceased to exist.

On the same land occupied by the Shakers now sits the home of the Abode of the Message, a community established in 1910 by the Indian Sufi master Pir-o-Murshid Hazrat Inayat Kan that was intended to help "unite humanity in brotherhood and wisdom." The Abode is the primary residence of the Sufi Order International, dedicated to honoring unity, truth and wisdom of all the world's religious traditions.

New Lebanon

Temperatures Rising

Early in 1820, a man by the name of John Kendall happened to buy a weather thermometer in a hardware store in his hometown of Worcester, Massachusetts. He noticed that it had a stamp on the back that assured him it was made in England. Something about this information bothered Mr. Kendall, and like all good inventors, he became mildly obsessed with the idea of making a better thermometer in America. He moved his family to New Lebanon and, after months of tinkering, opened a small factory to manufacture thermometers. It turned out that at first, Kendall's thermometer wasn't that different from the English model, but somehow, selling them locally to his friends and neighbors in hometown stores proved appealing to his proud customer base. But then something changed. Word got out that the Kendall thermometer was unbelievably accurate. Reportedly, people who bought and hung them in the same locale got the exact same temperature read as one another. How did he do it? Kendall kept that proprietary information to himself for some time, but eventually, he revealed his secret. Apparently what made the English thermometers less accurate was a tiny divider that regulated the mercury in the glass tube. Kendall invented a unique method that could eliminate the divider for absolute uniformity. Though Mr. Kendall died in 1831 at the age of forty-five, his sons, John and Edwin, took over the shop and added the manufacturing of aneroid barometers. Because his father had revealed his manufacturing secrets, competition reduced the company's profits, and it eventually closed.

7
Taghkanic

Rough and Ready

In simple appearances, Taghkanic looks merely like any other rural town with deep woods, thick forests and sloping terrain. What lies beneath the surface is fascinating. Taghkanic sits on some of the oldest rock in Columbia County and is rich with Mohican and Mohawk life that thrived in the hills. If you drive too fast on the Taconic Parkway, you might miss it, but you won't want to. Take the exit and stop. There is some type of strange energy in this sleepy town that pulls you in.

If you turn the clock back with a strong twist of the wrist, you will find the reason why this area is known as the High Taconics by geologists—its lands were formed by great slides of the Berkshire Mountains about 460 million years ago. Through this formation was the creation of great waterfalls and land so rugged that farmers could barely graze their sheep on it due to the immense amount of rock and thin soil. Despite these obstacles the land was claimed originally by the Livingston Manor in the late 1690s. Manors, as they were known, were run by lords who were granted privileges, much like lords of England. Like in England, lords got rich from collecting tax from their tenants, who paid high rents for poor conditions. In 1788, eight townships were established in the county. (Today there are eighteen.) One of these was named Livingston, comprising what are now Ancram, Copake, Gallatin and Taghkanic. Additional name changes occurred. Though the town was officially formed as "Granger" on March 19, 1803, the original

Hidden History of Columbia County, New York

Old 82, Taghkanic, New York. *Courtesy of Taghkanic town clerk.*

name was abandoned and changed to Taghkanic on March 25, 1814, and in 1824, the town was divided.

The town also shares its name with the Taconic Mountains, yet there are other explanations for the name Taghkanic. There's the theory that the Mohicans would hunt and camp near a local spring they called *Tok-kon'-nik*, said by some to signify "water enough" and by others to describe its ebb and flow or "come and go."

Of the meaning of the name, Dr. E.B. O'Callaghan wrote, "Tachanuk, 'Wood place,' literally 'the woods,' from *Takone*, 'forest,' and *iik*, 'place'." In places elsewhere in New York, the name *Taughannock* comes from the Algonquian-speaking Lenni-Lenape (Delaware) Indians, referring either to chief Taughannock or the word Taghkanic. No matter how you spell it, the unusual town of Taghkanic was born. In this area was a large lake that was originally known as Lake Charlotte, supposedly after the housekeeper working in Livingston's home there on the lavish and expansive Livingston Manor.

Big Chief, Little Chief

Taghkanic played a unique role in Columbia County's history when its citizens banded together to end what they called "the relic of Feudalism." With Livingston Manor controlling much of the county's lands and giving no ownership possibilities to its tenants, the people revolted in what was known as the Anti-Rent War of 1844. Spurred on by the successes of tenants in other parts of the county, in November of that year, the people formed the Taghkanic Mutual Association. The articles of incorporation pointed to the "great injustice of the present system of land ownership, permitting individuals to hold large tracks of land for which they have never, in essence, had rights to own." This was referring to the massive land grants rendered to Livingston, which gave him and his ancestors mass acreage in Columbia County. After pledging as a group not to pay rent to the Livingstons without the full backing of each member of the newly formed association, things took a strange turn of events.

The protestors in Taghkanic decided to organize themselves into tribes of "Indians" under the direction of two chiefs: Big Thunder, aka Smith A. Boughton, and Little Thunder, aka Mortimer C. Belding. Their roles, according to the pledge of the association, were to "forcibly resist the officers of the County in the discharge of their duties." The group of anti-rent activists gathered in their Indian costumes, which disguised the men completely and included animal skins and tails, horns, feathers and tin ornaments. Their faces were painted in red and black, as were their arms. They carried with them hatchets, pistols, spears, clubs and guns. In an elaborate display, the group paraded around in a marching assembly with one of its members playing a lone fife accompanied by a drum. Chief Big Thunder gave a speech about how horribly they had been wronged and the myriad injustices they had endured. They sang a song with lyrics vowing to resist. This group caused a great deal of excitement, and with so much violence already occurring in surrounding towns, most assumed the worst. The next month, in December 1844, the first conflict occurred when Sheriff Henry C. Miller went to Copake, a town neighboring Taghkanic, to serve processes and make a sale of property belonging to the disaffected parties. He arrived alone and was met by a force of 300 pseudo-Indians and another 1,500 people not in disguise. He was immediately captured by Big Thunder and 6 other chiefs who dragged him to a room, held a pistol to his side and burned the papers he was carrying. This action set off a chain reaction with the law seeking vindication with no limits. This did not dissuade the anti-rent protestors. In fact, Big Thunder made a date to speak at the tiny village of Smokey Hollow (now known as Hollowville in the town of Claverack). The legend of Big Thunder had spread tremendously within weeks, and hundreds of people attended the gathering.

Big Thunder arrived with a huge entourage. The chief and his accompanying pack made a rather colorful spectacle and, somehow in demonstrating their ability to use force, accidentally killed a man in the crowd by the name of W.H. Rifenburgh. When news of this reached the authorities that same day, the sheriff and his men made a decision to arrest Big Thunder before nightfall. By the time the sheriff arrived, the crowd had gone home, and the Indians were casually sitting around the Smokey Hollow tavern with their costumes removed. Arresting an unsuspecting Big Thunder came without a struggle at first. Big Thunder then tried to escape by drawing his pistol and summoning his soldiers. The sheriff, deputies and the Indian party fought fiercely, yet Big Thunder and Little Thunder were taken to prison in Hudson followed by a huge crowd. Lawyers for both sides assembled the next day, and throughout the county, a major protest among the anti-renters was brewing. So much concern prompted the courthouse to add extra security of added arms and ammunition for fear that there might be an attempt to rescue the prisoners. Troops of armed citizens did night watch, and the Hudson Light Guard patrolled with loaded muskets. Volunteers were stationed at the city bell as an alarm system in the event of intruders. A few days later, Attorney General Barker ordered one hundred men to be armed with an added four pieces of artillery.

With still more fears, the number was raised to five hundred men, called the Law and Order Association. The citizens of Hudson were notified by Governor Bouck that, for the first time in history, the city was being guarded by armed forces. He admonished the anti-rent protestors' rebellion and resistance to the law and told them that their safety was at risk because there were plans to rescue the ringleaders. A document signed by a number of well-known men of Hudson went out to the anti-rent protestors, warning them of the penalties if they continued to obstruct the law, yet men in disguise continued to fire on the lawmen and burn their papers. The fear and fighting went on for another month with even more military force. Yet Big Thunder and Little Thunder were eventually indicted and prosecuted, and a two-week trial ended in a "disagreement of the Jury." They were tried again months later by a different judge, and though convicted and confined in the Clinton County State Prison, they were given a pardon by the governor shortly after.

Taghkanic

Backwoods and Baskets

There's a theory that many of the tenant farmers on the Livingston Manor refusing to pay rent retreated to "the Hill" in Taghkanic, which was up a rocky slope reaching one thousand feet in elevation and overlooking Lake Charlotte (now Lake Taconic). This spot encompassed a sacred native outcropping called "signal rock"—the place where Mohicans would send smoke signals that could be seen throughout the county. These displaced people were originally from Palatine, Germany, forced out of their homelands, sent to America in 1710 and then shipped off from New Netherlands (New York City) to work as indentured servants on the Livingston Manor.

After retreating to Taghkanic, the group settled and possibly intermarried with the native Mohican Indians who also called Taghkanic their home.

The story is told that there is a map made in 1798 of people inhabiting the area with the names Propers and Dykemans. This was an isolated group of people who were shrouded in mystery. Members seemed to be difficult to identify and their skin color varied from light to dark to albino. They were storytellers, and up on the back roads of Taghkanic, they dug simple houses

Taghkanic Pondshiners family, Taghkanic, New York. *Courtesy of the Taghkanic town clerk.*

Hidden History of Columbia County, New York

Lake Charlotte Lakeside Club, Taghkanic, New York. *Collection of Jon and April Meredith, Kinderhook, New York.*

into the hillsides much like the Native Americans'. These people of the Hill were called Bushwhackers and Pondshiners.

They became known as Eastern Indian basket makers, and there's a theory that the name *Bushwhacker* was given because of the way that they would collect young white ash branches just before the appearance of the new moon and pound them in preparation for weaving baskets. The word *Bushwhacker* was already widespread in the early nineteenth century to reference backwoodsmen, or people who "beat the bush" in order to ambush their enemies. In the American Indian record gathered by Steven Pony Hill and sociologist Brewton Berry, the writers claim the Pondshiners were possibly tri-racial "isolates" mixing European Americans, African Americans and Native Americans.

Rumors surrounded Taghkanic backwoods clans. Their reclusiveness left the townspeople to create stories of witches and demons and peculiar mysteries of the outcasts. It's likely that many of these people simply lived in fear that they were always being followed. "The Frightened People" were referenced in many newspapers and books of the time warning how the clan would protect its privacy at all costs. As with all social outsiders, the Pondshiners were misunderstood. Both terms Bushwhacker and Pondshiner are considered slurs in most circumstances. Yet many similar outcast groups have existed in history, including the Moors of Delaware, who developed their own culture, and the Melungeons of Tennessee. Yet through their

Taghkanic

Original large Tagkhanic basket created by Bushwackers of Taghkanic. *Collection of Kurt and Janine Kilty, Chatham, Massachusetts.*

isolation and without worldly distractions, the Bushwhakers were productive in a unique way.

The baskets they made were legendary. In fact, few are in general circulation today, and most exist only in well-guarded antique collections. Though the quality of the baskets made them popular in the 1840s, the Bushwhacker baskets were mostly sold in local hardware stores and by the side of the road in West Taghkanic. On occasion, one of the Pondshiners might carry the baskets on long poles and travel on foot selling the baskets from town to town.

As many as forty families made baskets on the Hill over a span of 100 to 150 years. Yet the quality, uniqueness, elegance and workmanship are uncannily consistent.

These were people who kept to themselves, had no use for outsiders and often married within their own families. Therefore, they didn't travel and would make use of whatever variety of tree they had at their disposal when making their magnificent baskets. The style of basket they created was known as the swing-handle basket. It was quite utilitarian, as one could just as easily use it to pick blueberries as to decorate a dining table. The baskets held water, were lightweight and stacked well one on top of another. To the untrained eye, these baskets might seem uncomplicated, yet in reality, they were quite sophisticated. The Bushwhacker baskets were often confused with the Shaker baskets of Mount Lebanon, whose workmanship and simplicity have earned them worldwide recognition as well. The Shakers actually purchased baskets from the Bushwhackers for use in addition to making their own baskets. Though similar, the baskets have distinguishing traits. The Bushwhackers made one type of basket for many uses, and the Shakers made different types baskets for specific uses.

Whether the Pondshiners still exist is a mystery. Lake Taconic has many mapped trails, road and paths for hiking. Yet there are many unmarked trails shown on no map that lead into forgotten and foreboding foothills.

Red with Rage

The name Proper comes up again in Taghkanic's hidden history in one of the town's most notorious headlines. On September 12, 1879, Henry Moett committed a double murder taking the life of his wife, Isabel, and that of her paramour, Jacob "Red-Headed Jake" Proper. It was called one of the most revolting murders ever committed in Columbia County. Retold in the *National Police Gazette* at the time of his sentencing in New York on February 28, 1880, the crime took place in the village of Churchtown in the town of Taghkanic. The scene of the crime was the Moett house, which was located deep in Taghkanic's rugged woods. Moett's wife, Isabel, was from the Williams family, who were also from Taghkanic, and her marriage to Henry was her second. She was ten years his senior at forty-one years old. There was doubt as to whether the couple was ever officially married.

Jake Proper was the son of John Proper of Hudson and was just twenty-five. Apparently, the young Proper had moved into the Moett house, displacing Henry, who took to sleeping in the barn while Jake slept with his wife in his bed. This went on for about two months until Moett's wife demanded Henry leave or she would call the police.

In the court papers, Henry reported that the two were on "intimate terms," and this enraged him. He did, however, plan to leave on the day of the tragedy. On September 12, Moett quarreled with his wife, and Jake interceded, demanding that Henry leave or he would "take out his heart."

During the fight Henry apparently thought Jake was reaching for a weapon, but before he could, Henry pulled out a pistol and shot Jake once in the chest. As he was falling, Henry shot him again. Jake ran for the woods, and Henry shot him three more times. While the murder of her lover was taking place, Isabel ran for the house. Henry reloaded his five-chamber pistol and pursued her to their home. Emptying his pistol at close range, he shot his wife dead. After resting his dead wife's body on their bed, Henry rode on horseback to Chatham Village, where he surrendered to Deputy Sheriff Smith and confessed to the crime. His final quote was "I think the law will justify me in what I did, and I have no regrets." Apparently, Jake Proper survived the attack by crawling out of the woods and finding his way to a neighboring farmer's barn, where he died two days later. Henry Moett was convicted of murder in the first degree and was hanged on March 15, 1880, in the public square in Hudson.

Bare Knuckles in Boston Corners

Boston Corners is an odd name for a place in New York. Currently it's a hamlet of the town of Ancram in Columbia County. Yet the strange story of Boston Corners starts back in 1851, when this tract of land, about one thousand acres in total, was originally part of the Massachusetts commonwealth that eventually ceded to the state of New York after a bloody, bare-knuckled brawl at an illegal prize fight between John Morrisey and Yankee Sullivan.

Because this bit of land was nestled on the west side of the challenging terrain of the Taconic Mountain Range, just a short distance from East Taghkanic in Columbia County, it was out of reach for Massachusetts lawmen, and given its isolation, it attracted the worst of the worst. Among the outlaws who congregated there were gamblers, thieves and men who reportedly would dye losing racehorses so they could be raced under another name. It also attracted boxers because throughout the state, the violent sport was outlawed.

The fight between Morrisey and Sullivan changed Boston Corners forever. In 1853, Morrisey, the young fighter from Troy, New York, accepted a challenge to fight the older Yankee Sullivan at Boston Corners. The site was chosen because of its reputation for corruption.

Hidden History of Columbia County, New York

Yankee Sullivan prizefighter, 1846. *Courtesy of the Library of Congress.*

It also happened to be the first stop on the New York Harlem Railroad running directly into town.

On the outside, this fight would seem like a mismatch. Morrisey was just twenty-two years old, some eighteen years younger than the forty-year-old Sullivan. The height and weight differentials were also unbalanced with Morrisey at six feet, two inches tall and 175 pounds and Sullivan a mere 140 pounds and somewhat shorter. The promoters of the day did a spectacular job attracting thousands of spectators who traveled on foot, by horseback, by carriage and by train to drink in the streets, raise hell and celebrate the prize-fighting spectacle. Newspaper reports stated that the crowd was rowdy and that the fight got ugly fast. The two men gutted it out in a virtual bloodbath that continued for an incredible thirty-seven unrelenting rounds, and eventually the affair erupted in a riot with Sullivan jumping into the crowd to brawl with the fans. When Sullivan exited the ring, the officials raised Morrisey's arm and declared him the winner. Just as the fight ended, the authorities from Massachusetts showed up and arrested Morrisey while Sullivan escaped.

After this hellish episode, the citizens of Boston Corners petitioned New York State and the U.S. Congress to allow the town to become part of New York. On January 3, 1855, Boston Corners officially became part of Columbia County with more regular law enforcement bringing order to the town.

8
VALATIE

Although neighboring Kinderhook had been thriving with settlements since Hudson landed in the early 1600s, nearby Vaaltje, the early Dutch name or today, Valatie, was still uncharted territory. Today it's a small town with a strange name, but it has a rather alluring past. In an area along the Kinderhook Creek east of the village was a trail known as the Great New England Path. It is believed that this may have been the spot that Jan Hendrickes de Bruyn was given a patent in 1679 for Pompenick. This was the name of the local Indian sachem whose name meant "pumpkin field," though some think Pompenick may have meant "playing field" as well. The land patent offered an acreage spreading from the Valatie Kill east to a rock cliff called the "Offgevallenbergh." The Valatie Kill is an outlet off Kinderhook Lake that cuts through Valatie Village, creating several spectacular waterfalls that later businesses used for power. The original *Vaaltje* Dutch translation of Valatie means "little falls."

It was also known as *Pachaquack*—the Mohican word for "cleared meadow"—which appeared on an early 1686 map of the area, pointing to a meeting place for the Mohican people who lived along the banks of Valatie Kill and Kinderhook Creek. According to Collier's *History of Old Kinderhook*, the area was just south of the "Great Fish Lake," Vak Lak according to the Mohicans, now known as Kinderhook Lake.

The Native Americans' influence was seen throughout the town. Pompoonick University, or "the school in the woods," was an ancient one-room schoolhouse named for the Indian Pompoen, who owned the land in

Island No. 10 on the Beaver Kill, Valatie, New York. *Collection of Jon and April Meredith, Kinderhook, New York.*

Wheeler's Feed Store, Upper Main Street, Valatie, New York. *Collection of Jon and April Meredith, Kinderhook, New York.*

the seventeenth century. From its inception in 1830 and during the 1880s, up to fifty students crowded into this tight space to be taught by female teacher being paid probably seven dollars per week. Needless to say, the town had trouble keeping teachers.

WILD AND THE WATERING HOLES

The town has also been known as Millville. Attracted to the area because of the immense waterfall that curved through the town, those seeking prosperity in manufacturing started large cotton and gristmills. Nathan Wild (1790–1867) was one of the original cotton mill owners. He came from Manchester, England, and built his mill in 1829.

In Wild's knitting mill, a young worker by the name of Elizabeth A. Hawyer died after holding the yarn in her mouth and poisoning herself via an open cold sore. She was only fifteen years old. Wild was considered one of the early founders of Valatie, having

Nathan Wild, portrait. *From* The History of Columbia County, *author's collection.*

arrived in the early 1800s. Along with the mill, he designed and constructed a Federal-style home where he and his wife, Sarah, raised nine children. One of Wild's employees built a brilliant loom. Recognizing his genius, Wild gave him leave to start his own business, in which he miraculously manufactured the very first machine gun. Rensselear Reynolds might have been famous had the military accepted this weapon into its arms; however, it rejected it at the time, and Reynolds returned to the mills unheralded for his invention.

Mills, hard spirits and worker rivalry went hand in hand in early towns like Valatie. The problem of drinking was recorded in the *Columbia Washington* on May 11, 1843, which included a study of the tavern keepers in the

United States Hotel at the turn of the century, Valatie, New York. *Collection of Jon and April Meredith, Kinderhook, New York.*

township between 1790 and 1843 by the town's local men Dr. H.L. Van Dyck and General Charles Whiting. They concluded that fifty-five of the tavern keepers were drunks and twenty were hard drinkers. Additionally, one out of six of their children became alcoholics. Despite the temperance movement and until Prohibition, drinking in Valatie was on the rise. The drink of choice was rye, but beer and whiskey rose in popularity when Irish workers arrived. Alcohol, like whiskey, was cheap—only twenty-five cents a gallon throughout the nineteenth century—and rum, made locally in Massachusetts, was practically free. This encouraged men to drink in bars, where women were not welcomed. Drinking and brawling made the news frequently in Valatie with fistfights and bloodshed rolling out onto the main streets. In the 1870s, the number of establishments where men could drink reached into the double digits. Even when Prohibition began, it did little to curb the consuming habits of Valatiens with laws that no one enforced.

The lively little town of Valatie offered its many villagers outstanding entertainment, such as the Valatie Opera House, where shows and events occurred nightly. One of the early establishments that drew people together to meet, socialize and sip spirits was the United States Hotel. At the hotel, Madame Norman, a celebrated astrologist, held court.

Valatie

Fighting Words

Just a few feet away from the hotel was where the official boxing matches took place at the Valatie Opera House. Whether an opera was actually ever performed here is a mystery, yet in 1929 and the early 1930s, Valatie featured Friday night bouts bringing local talent to town to take part in "the art of the squared circle" with names like Kid Minor, Boggie Jim, Buffalo Bucker and Baby Face Jones. George (Bucky) Everett, who was the co-proprietor of Bucky and Hal's Restaurant, was one of several local Valatiens to promote boxing programs in the area. The announcer was Chatham's "leather-lunged" shoe salesman, J. Edward Brown, who called the fights in Valatie's smoke-filled Opera House. Several contenders battled it out in Valatie hoping to make the big-time boxing venues, though many of the bouts were staged. A local favorite was Charlie Coley, who fought under the name Kid Chocolate. As the story goes, "the Kid" didn't have a proper pair of boxing trunks but was kindly supplied with a pair of women's panties by his buddies at the local Manny-Reilly Mill. Apparently, the trunks brought him more cheers from the fans than did his boxing skills. One particular night, the Kid was fighting, and before the fight could finish, his pretty pair of pants split wide open, causing the referee to call the bout a draw. Women screamed and the men in the audience laughed when so much of the Kid was exposed.

Valatie Main Street in the mid-nineteenth century. *Collection of Jon and April Meredith, Kinderhook, New York.*

Old St. Nick

So no one thinks that Valatie was all about drinking and brawling, there were some very good and charitable things that happened in this very tiny town on a very big waterfall. Santa himself was central in the historic pages of the Valatie storybook. The first Santa Claus Club in the country was formed in Valatie in 1946 by fifteen former soldiers who used their military pay to bring gifts and holiday cheer to families who were suffering due to the closure of nearby clothing mills. The concept has spread to other communities around the country. The Valatie club still exists and holds a parade on the Main Street at precisely 3:30 p.m. every Christmas Eve.

Santa Claus holds another piece of Valatie's hidden history. Virginia O'Hanlon Douglas died on May 13, 1971, at the age of eighty-one, in a nursing home in Valatie, New York, and is buried in the Chatham Rural Cemetery. It turns out that Virginia was the world-famous eight-year-old little girl who wrote a letter asking, "Is There a Santa Claus?" The reply came from an editorial in the *New York Sun* written by Francis P. Church and was titled "Yes, Virginia, There Is a Santa Claus," dated Tuesday, September 21, 1897. This editorial ran each year in newspapers across the country and in the *Sun* until it went out of business in 1949. How did Virginia find her way to Valatie? As reported in the *New York Times* by Manny Fernandez, on Christmas Eve 2010, Virginia had lived most of her life in New York City as a school teacher, but when she became ill, she moved in with her only daughter in North Chatham. Rumor is she liked that the town still honored Santa Claus—Virginia responded to letters about her own famous letter throughout her entire life. Jim Temple, her grandson who lived in Valatie, and several other relatives still tell Virginia's story, lecturing around the country free of charge. They all still believe in Santa Claus.

Feminine Mystique

The women of Valatie held secrets. Here are a few of the lesser-known publicized truths.

Though thousands of women like Elizabeth Cady Stanton, Susan B. Anthony and others lined up in New York during the late 1800s to petition for women's rights, one woman did not: the wife of New York governor

Martin Henry Glynn, (1871–1924) a prominent hometown favorite resident of Valatie, New York.

Glynn was born in Valatie in 1871, the son of a saloon owner. He grew up living above one of the town's famous Irish pubs on Main Street. He graduated from Fordham University in New York City and passed the bar. Instead of entering law, he became a journalist. He became editor and then owner of the *Albany Times Union.*

In 1914, a huge suffrage march began in New York City. The women traveled on foot all the way to Albany, New York, with the intention of asking then New York State governor Martin Glynn to appoint poll watchers in the 1915 suffrage referendum. Oddly enough, Governor Glynn supported suffrage, but apparently, his wife, Mary Magrane Glynn, was opposed. Under pressure, Governor Glynn refused to speak at a suffrage meeting, and attendees threatened that when it came time for him to run, they would ruin him. Apparently, Mary Magrane Glynn was listed as vice-president in the Women's Anti-Suffrage Association in Albany. Clearly, suffrage was a complicated matter at the time, and perhaps to keep the peace in this instance, Governor Glynn sided with his wife.

While Glynn somehow survived this event and enjoyed a long and successful political career, he sadly came to a strange and heart-wrenching ending. Suffering from chronic back pain from a spinal injury throughout his adult life, Glynn committed suicide in 1924. He was buried at the St. Agnes Cemetery in Menands, New York. In her bequest of 1946, his wife, Mary left funds for the construction of the library at the Martin H. Glynn High School in Valatie.

WOMEN'S FARM FOR REFORM

The remainder of Valatie's secrets surrounding women seem to be squarely situated on a prime three-hundred-acre parcel of land that was deemed a suitable location for a women's prison in 1908. It seems that the New York State Farm for women was a bit of an experiment in creating a custodial-type prison for older women who had repeatedly committed petty crimes. Before the prison in Valatie was built, women who were arrested for prostitution or drunkenness were sent to local jails. These women presented a problem for society, and while the local authorities were less concerned with reforming them, they were extremely concerned with keeping them off the streets. This action was led by a group in the purity movement in the early 1900s called the Women's Prisons Association of New York (WPANY). In essence, this was their way of engaging a method of eugenics (the science of improving the human population by controlled breeding for increased desirable characteristics). The women of WPANY worried that these female criminals, many of whom were immigrants, would negatively influence the morals of society. Their intention was to indefinitely incarcerate the women by creating laws through the State Farm Bill. Within the new legislation provisions, $100,000 was allocated to build an innovative institution that would offer outdoor work for the inmates, thus the establishment would become self-supporting through farming. The prison was designed originally to hold five hundred women with multiple buildings on a huge campus. It was built just one and a half miles from the town of Valatie with John Mealy, a local resident, appointed as warden.

The original idea was to create a model prison with several luxurious cottages, a recreation hall and ample outdoor activities, suitable for farming and gardening. The model prison would also have occupational instruction that would ultimately improve the lives of those incarcerated. Yet in reality, when the women started to arrive at the farm in 1914, there was but one small cottage available to hold about sixty people in total. A second cottage on the farm was designated and built exclusively for the warden. Despite a positive report in the *She Hudson Evening Register* on Friday, January 22, 1915, which painted a pleasant picture of the farm as a success with twenty-four inmates doing light farm work, the number of inmates grew rapidly, resulting in over eighty women living in one small cottage by 1917. The profile of the criminals was usually women over the age of thirty who were not insane and had been found guilty of misdemeanor or lesser crimes at least five times in two years. During the overcrowding years, seventeen tried to escape, but only three succeeded. The model correctional facility accepted women who were more hardened criminals as prisons in the state made room for the growing number of men who needed a lockup. But in just one short year, the prison saw a rapid decline and was turned over to the State Health Department to be used as a facility for women with venereal disease.

Houdini—Who Dun It?

According to a firsthand account in the *Chatham Courier* in 1955, Harry Houdini Pictures came to Valatie in the early 1920s to film a movie. Few knew at the time that it would be his last picture. According to reports, the film was held up for three months while the producers looked for a suitable waterway where they could film Houdini's amazing escape. When reports leaked of Houdini's film plans, huge crowds gathered in Valatie as Houdini and his entourage rolled into town.

The production crew erected a huge waterwheel just near Valatie's covered bridge where the water was dammed on the raging Kinderhook Creek. The

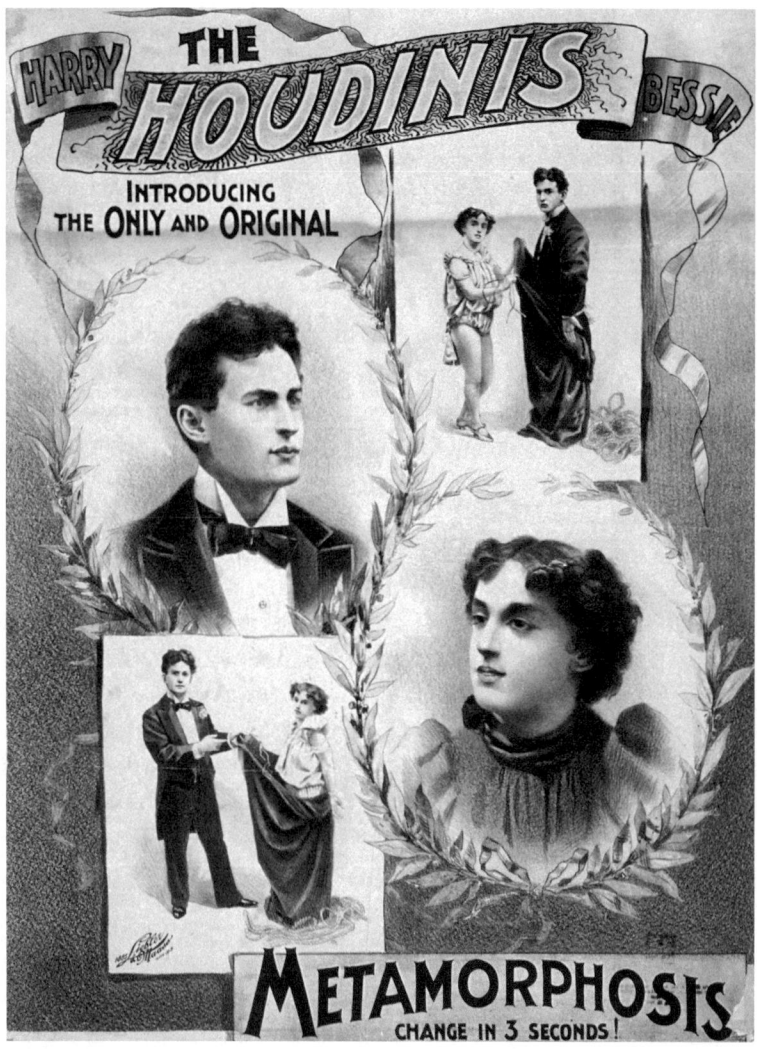

Harry and Bessie Houdini promotional poster, 1895. *Courtesy of the Library of Congress.*

work of constructing the huge wheel was done under the direction of Floyd Buckley of Chatham, who was part of the Houdini Troupe. During filming, the crew stayed in Chatham's Stanwix Hotel. The highlight was, of course, Houdini's ability to miraculously avoid disaster with magical maneuvers. During the big escape scene, the great magician was tied to the wheel, and as the wheel was set in motion, Houdini miraculously escaped by plunging into the deep and rapidly flowing waters below. The film was called *Haldane of the Secret Service*. During its filming, papers as far away as Poughkeepsie ran stories about Houdini's work in the tiny town of Valatie. Despite Houdini's great film successes to this point, *Haldane* was a total flop. Some say the film failed because Houdini was sadly depressed and preoccupied. Few know that Harry Houdini was obsessed with speaking with the dead. He favored séances and made many attempts at reaching spirits from the beyond. When his efforts failed, he became outraged with those within the Spiritualist movement who claimed they had successfully made contact with the dead.

Harry Houdini became Spiritualism's greatest antagonist. He was born Erich Weiss in Budapest, Hungary, in 1874, the son of a rabbi. His family immigrated to America in 1878. Houdini began performing at the age of nine with a trapeze act and then magic. In 1893, he began experimenting with the escape arts. Houdini became widely known as the "Handcuff King," and in 1900, he toured England, Scotland, the Netherlands, Germany, France and Russia. With his success, his interests expanded, and in 1918, he signed a film contract and went to Hollywood. In the 1920s, after the death of his mother, Cecilia, he turned his interest toward communicating with her in the afterlife and eventually to debunking the claims of Spiritualist mediums. Unlike the failed attempts of scientists and academics who tried to expose these frauds, Houdini felt that his unique training as a magician gave him the ability to see through a medium's tricks and deceptive acts. Soon after *Haldane* bombed at the box office, Houdini left filmmaking for good and returned to stage shows. His making of the film at Valatie's Beaver Kill Creek proved to be a fateful plunge that left him without an escape.

BIBLIOGRAPHY

Chatham Courier *articles retrieved from Fultonhistory.com*

Albany Times Union. "Night of Carnage." December 28, 1986.

Almshouse. http://en.wikipedia.org/wiki/Almshouse (accessed February 13, 2014).

Amelinckx, Andrew. "Do You Believe in Ghosts?" *Hudson-Catskill*, March 14, 2011.

Ancestry.com. http://archiver.rootsweb.ancestry.com/th/read/Melungeon/2003-03/1047772146.

Andrews, Deming Edward, and Faith Andrews. *Work and Worship Among the Shakers: Their Craftmanship and Economic Order.* Toronto, ON: General Publishing Company Ltd., 1974, 157–58.

Baker, Jean H. *Margaret Sanger: A Life of Passion.* New York: Hill and Wang, 2011, 25–27.

Barbor, Hugh, Arthur Worrall and Christopher Densmore. *Quaker Crosscurrents: Three Hundred Years of Friends in the New York Yearly Meetings.* Syracuse, NY: Syracuse University Press, 1995.

Bibliography

"Biography: American Shaker Founder 'Mother' Ann Lee 1736–1784." http://b-womeninamericanhistory18.blogspot.com/search/label/Biography%20-%20Mother%20Ann%20Lee (accessed September 2013).

Bolton, Matthew J. "*The Red Badge of Courage* in the Context of the 1890s." *Critical Insights on Stephen Crane*. Edited by Eric Carl Link. Pasadena, CA: Salem, 2010.

Boot and Shoe Recorder. "How a New York Village Got Rid of the Name Given It by a Peddler." September 18, 1901, 139.

Bradbury, Anna R. *History of the City of Hudson, New York: Biographical Sketches of Henry Hudson and Robert Fulton*. Hudson, NY: Record Printing, 1908.

Broderick, Warren. "A Grim Story." *Pittstown Centinel*, May 11, 1976.

Brody, Catherine Tyler (town historian 1993–2001). "A Brief History of Gallatin." Gallatin-ny.com, 5–6.

Buckland, Raymond. *The Spirit Book: Encyclopedia of Clairvoyance, Channeling and Spirit Communication*. Canton, MI: Visible Ink Press, 2005, 119.

Burba, Howard. "The Abduction of Angeline Stewart." *Dayton Daily News*, December 3, 1933.

Burnell, Edna. "Do Columbia County Spirits Walk When the Moon Is New?" *Chatham Courier*, October 22, 1936.

Cambridge Tribune, June 20, 1919.

Chatham Courier. "Boxing Reigned as Chatham Area's Leading Sport, Top Cards Offered." March 5, 1964.

———. "Century Ago, Six Farmers Once Owned Land Chatham Village." April 26, 1956.

———. "Chas Van Buren Attended Quaker Sunday School. Lived in Ghent House Where Runaway Slaves Were Hidden." May 17, 1928.

Bibliography

———. "Edna St. Vincent Millay, America's Foremost Poetess, Tells in Exclusive Interview Her Fondness for Columbia Count and Other Interesting Things." October 6, 1927.

———. "1882 Killing Recalled. Unearth Human Bones at Austerlitz Murder Site." November 10, 1958.

———. "End of Claverack Legend: A New Book Reveals a Visit from St. Nicholas Was Not Written in Columbia County. " December 8, 1957.

———. "Friends Meeting House in Rayville to Be Restored" March 1, 1956, 1–2.

———. "Forgotten Graveyard Recalls Days When Slavery Flourished in Old Kinderhook." January 14, 1960.

———. "Holmes Places Millay Among the World's Great." 1931.

———. "Houdini Picture at Local Theater. Scenes Taken at Valatie." December 1923.

———. "Hudson Resident, 89, Recalls Hanging of Oscar Beckwith, the Austerlitz Murderer." January 28, 1954.

———. "Millay Ashes Have Not Been Interred." June 28, 1951.

———. "No Bottom Pond. Yesteryear's Farmers Knew of Death Lurking Beneath Sparkling Jewel of Pond in Austerlitz Hills." April 28, 1960.

———. "Noted Poetess Announces New Work in Statement to *Courier*." August 2, 1928.

———. "Poet Reports German Ship off Tortola." March 21, 1940.

———. "Spelunkers Probe Austerlitz Cave, Fail to Find Cat." September 27, 1956.

———. "Stovepipe Alley. Forgotten, Forlorn and Forbidding Colony." May 1, 1958.

Bibliography

———. "To Establish a Knitting Plant in the Windsor Hotel." November 10, 1921.

———. "Veteran Actor Recalls One of Houdini's Escapes at Valatie." March 24, 1955.

———. "What Water Shortage? Canaan Dowser Claims Chatham and Hudson Are Located atop Large Underground River." January 16, 1964.

Chatham Courier County Fair Edition. "Canaan Dowser Can Find Water by Running His Hand over Map." August 23, 1931.

Chester (Pennsylvania) Times, February 24, 1885.

Claverack New York. http://www.revolutionaryday.com/usroute9/claverack (accessed September 5, 2013).

Collier, Edward A., DD. *The History of Old Kinderhook from Aboriginal Times to Present Time.* New York: G.P. Putnam's Sons, 1914, 158.

———. "Native Americans of Columbia County Kinderhook and Its Indians." In *A History of Old Kinderhook.* New York: Putnam's Sons, 1914, 8–21.

Cooney, Michael. "Harvey Mountain and the Tale of Lost Gold." http://upstateearth.blogspot.com/2012/05/harvey-mountain-and-tale-of-lost-gold.html, May 1, 2012 (accessed September 2, 2013).

Cronan, William. *Changes in the Land: Indians, Colonists, and the Ecology of New England.* New York: Hill and Wang, 1983.

Dahlgren, Peter, and Colin Sparks, eds. *Journalism and Popular Culture.* London: Sage Publications, 1992, 175.

Daily (Hudson, NY) Register. "The Canaan Affair." April 14, 1868.

The Delsarte Project. http://www.delsarteproject.com/?A_Brief_History_of_Delsarte. Last updated February 20, 2014. (Accessed December 23, 2013).

Bibliography

Dictionary.com, s.v. "Alienist." http://dictionary.reference.com/browse/alienist (accessed December 2013).

Ellis, Captain Franklin. *The History of Columbia County, New York*. Philadelphia: Everts & Ensign, 1878.

Epstein, Daniel. *"What Lips My Lips Have Kissed": The Loves and Love Poems of Edna St. Vincent Millay*. New York: Henry Holt & Co., 2001, 250–53.

Etymology Dictionary, s.v. "Alien." http://www.etymonline.com/index.php?term=alien (accessed December 2013).

Faber, Harold. "Hudson Casts a New Light on Its Red-Light Past." New York Times, October 21, 1994.

Fernandez, Manny. "To Virginia's Family, Yes, Santa Claus Is Still Real." *New York Times*, December 24, 2010.

"First Lady: Hannah Van Buren." National First Ladies Library. http://www.firstladies.org/biographies/firstladies.aspx?biography=8 (accessed August 20, 2013).

Fisher, Donald W., and Stephen L. Nightingale. *The Rise and Fall of the Taconic Mountains: A Geological History of Eastern New York*. Hensonville, NY: Black Dome Press Corp., 2006, 4–5.

Flannery, Michael. *Civil War Pharmacy: A History of Drug, Drug Supply, and Provision, and Therapies for the Union and Confederacy*. New York: Hawthorn Press, Inc., 2004, 31.

Foster, Lawrence. *Women, Family, and Utopia: Communal Experiments of the Shakers, the Oneida Community and the Mormons*. Syracuse, NY: Syracuse University Press, 1991, 23–24.

French, J.H., and R.P. Smith. *Gazetteer of the State of New York*. Syracuse, NY: R. Pearsall Smith, 1860, 24.

Bibliography

Gale, Daniel. *A Sketch of Lebanon Springs: Its Attractions as a Summer Resort—A Visit to the Shakers—History of the Town—Columbia Hall—Railroad Guide, etc*. Pittsfield, MA: Gale Daniel, Chickering & Axell, Printers, 1872, 5.

Gazetteer and Business Directory of Columbia County. Syracuse, NY: Hamilton Child, 1871–72, 184.

Grumet, Robert Steven. *The Lenapes: Indians of North America*. London: Chelsea House Pub, 1989.

Gullason, Thomas A. "Stephen Crane at Claverack College: A New Reading." *Syracuse University Surface/ Courier*, October 1, 1992.

Hall, Bruce Edward. *Diamond Street: The Story of the Little Town With the Big Red Light District*. Hensonville, NY: Black Dome Press Corp., 1994.

Hamilton, Allan McLane. *The Intimate Life of Alexander Hamilton: Based Chiefly upon Original Family Letters and Other Documents, Many of Which Have Never Been Published*. New York: Charles Scribner's Sons, 1910, 180.

Harnagel, Chris Andrew, and Sherman Chauncy Bishop. *The Mastodons, Mammoths and Other Pleistocene Mammals of New York State*. Albany: State University of New York Press, 1922, 22–23.

Hauk, Dennis William. *Haunted Places: The National Directory of Ghostly Abodes, Sacred Sites*. New York: Penguin Books, 1994, 291.

Higgins, Patrick. "Battle of Boston Corners." All About Town. http://abouttown.us/index.php/all-abouttown-articles/local-history/936-The-Battle-of-Boston-Corners (accessed, January 14, 2014).

Hoffman, George Nile. "No Bottom Pond's Mystery Has Never Been Solved." *Chatham Courier*, August 1928.

Hudson Library. http://hudsonarealibrary.org/about-us/history-of-the-library-building (accessed October 19, 2013).

Hughes, Charles H., MD. "The Alienist and Neurologist." *A Journal of Scientific, Clinical and Forensic Neurology and Psychology, Psychiatry and Neuriatry* 22, no. 1 (1906): 465.

BIBLIOGRAPHY

Hurd, Henry M. *The Institutional Care of the Insane in the United State and Canada*. Vol. 4. Baltimore, MD: Johns Hopkins Press, 1916–17, 527–28.

Johannes, Wilhelmus Wessels. *History of the Roman-Dutch Law*. Grahamstown, Cape Colony: African Book Company, Limited, 1908, 100.

"John P. Clum—The Early Years." Retrieved October 19, 2011. http://en.wikipedia.org/wiki/John_Clum.

Kearns, Marguerite. "The Strange Story of the Governor's Wife." Posted January 3, 2013. http://www.suffragewagon.org/?p=5661 (accessed November 1, 2013).

Keeney, John. "Sports Shorts: The Lost Art." *Chatham Courier*, February 2, 1950.

"Kinderhook Village a Bicentennial Community, January 1976." Kinderhook Village Bicentennial Committee, July 4, 1976.

KLC website. http://kinderhooklakecorp.org/wp-content/uploads/2012/01/KLC-Electric-Park.pdf (accessed November 2013.)

Ledoux, Gary Nantan. *The Life and Times of John P. Clum*. Vol. 1. Claverack, NY: Tombstone Trafford Publishing, 2007.

Letter written by the City Library of Poughkeepsie to Clarence Shepherd. New York, January 15, 1934.

"Martin Van Buren." http://en.wikipedia.org/wiki/Martin_Van_Buren (accessed December 23, 2013).

Millay, Norma, ed. *Collected Poems by Edna St. Vincent Millay*. New York: Harper Collins, 1956.

Miller, B.S. *Columbia County at the End of the Century: A Historical Record of Its Formation and Settlement, Its Resources, Its Institutions, and Its People*. Hudson, NY: Record Printing and Publishing Co., 1900.

Miller, M. Stephen. *Inspired Innovations: A Celebration of Shaker Ingenuity*. Lebanon, NH: University Press of New England, 2010, 145–57.

Bibliography

Miller, Stephen B. *Historical Sketches of Hudson: Embracing the Settlement of the City, City Government, Business Enterprises, Churches, Press, Schools, Libraries, &C.* Hudson, NY: Bryan and Weber Printers, 1862, 52–55.

Moore, Stanley E. "A Cave That Might Change the New York State Thruway Plans." *National Speleological Society News* 15, no. 1 (January 1957): 7.

Mossman, F. Carol. "Violent Winds, Rain Burst Philmont Dam in '38, Caused $100,000 Damage." *Chatham Courier*, September 30, 1965.

Mt. Lebanon Herb Festival. http://www.mountlebanonherbfest.com/herb-history (accessed, November 2, 2013).

"A Muslim in Victorian America: The Life or Alexander Russell Webb." *Antiques Magazine* (January 2004): 68.

Myers, Arthur. "The Brawls at Boston Corners." *Sports Illustrated Vault*, April 2, 1973. http://sportsillustrated.cnn.com/vault/article/magazine/MAG1087215/2/index.htm (accessed February 14, 2014).

Our Lady of Lourdes Grotto. http://catholicplaces.net/lebanonH.htm (accessed January 12, 2014).

Phrenological Journal and Science of Health 60–61 (1839): 304.

Pitt, David E. "A Gala for Oliver North Without the Honoree." Special to *New York Times*, August 16, 1987.

Rafter, Nicole Hahn. *Justice: Women, Prison and Social Control.* New Brunswick, NJ: Transaction Publishers, 1990, 94–95.

Register Star, January 6, 1991.

Reiber, Allison. "44 Obscure Facts You Didn't Know About US Presidents." Mashable, July 4, 2013. http://mashable.com/2013/07/04/us-presidents-fun-facts (accessed November 28, 2013).

Ruttenber, Edward Manning. *Footprints of the Red Men Indian Geographical Names in the Valley of Hudson's River, the Valley of the Mohawk and on the Delaware, Their*

Bibliography

Location and the Probable Meaning of Some of Them. N.p.: Forgotten Books, 2013. Originally published 1906 in Proceedings of the New York State Historical Association. Seventh-annual meeting, with constitution, bylaws and list of members.

Schram, Margaret. *Claverack Township: The History and Heritage*. Claverack, NY: Town of Claverack Historical Society, 1976. Reprinted, 1983.

Seaman, Tobias. "The Lost Pondshiners." http://www.themorningnews.org/article/the-lost-pondshiners.

Sedgwick, Maria Catharine. "Slavery in New England." *Bentley's Miscellany* 34 (1853): 417–24. Retrieved August 2010.

Shepard, Clarence D. *History of Rayville*. Pittsfield, MA: privately printed, 1937.

Shew, Joel, MD. *Hydrotherapy: The Water-Cure; Its Principles, Modes of Treatment, &c.* New York: Wiley and Putnam, 1844, 31–33.

Shprintzen, Adam D. *The Vegetarian Crusade: The Rise of an American Reform Movement, 1817–1921*. Chapel Hill: University of North Carolina Press, 2013, 55.

Sketches of New Lebanon. http://www.archive.org/stream/sketchoflebanons00gale/sketchoflebanons00gale_djvu.txt (accessed December 3, 2013).

Special from Gravenhurst, Tornonto, to the *Daily Register*.

Starna, William A. *From Homeland into New Land: A History of the Mahican Indians, 1600–1830*. Lincoln: University of Nebraska Press, 90.

Streeter, Ed. "Deathly Noises at Claverack: The Hangman's Tree." *Chatham Courier*, June 27, 1957.

Testimonials of the Life, Character, Revelations and Doctrines of Mother Ann Lee, and the Elders with Her, Through Whom the Word of the Eternal Life Was Opened in This Day of Christ's Second Appearing. Albany, NY: Weed, Parsons & Co., Printers, 1888, 16–18.

BIBLIOGRAPHY

Thesing, William B. *Reading the Socioeconomic Roles of Millay's Daily Life: The Servant Problem and the Men Working*. Columbia: University of South Carolina, 1931, 43.

Thomas, Eileen. "The *Hudson Gazette* Editor in 1824 was a Bright Young Lawyer Named John W. Edmonds." *Chatham Courier*, June 23, 1949.

———. "Tales of Old Columbia." *Chatham Courier*, June 10, 1948.

Trenton (New Jersey) Times, February 24, 1885.

Turtle, Jedi. "2.1-Mile Snowshoe to No Bottom Pond." Sunday, January 10, 2010. http://jedi-turtle.blogspot.com/2010/01/2.html (accessed, August 1, 2013).

Ulmer, Stephen. "Mountain Ten, Austerlitz, NY, 1948–1978." http://www.nelsap.org/ny/mt10.html (accessed October 10, 2013).

Valatie Times/New York Daily Times, March 8, 1854.

Valatievillage.com (accessed December 2, 2013).

Van de Water, Frederic Franklyn. *Grey Riders: the Story of the New York State Troopers*. New York: MacMillan, 1922, 243.

Varney, J.M. *Oscar Fitzallan Beckwith*. Hillsdale, NY: Harbinger Print, 1890.

Vickery, Gladys. "Brainard: Indians and Quakers Frequented This Once Thriving, Now Placid, Dorment Community." *Chatham Courier*, January 19, 1967.

———. "Red Rock. Stockbridge Indians Once Camped along Stream That Flows through Tiny Hamlet." Chatham Courier, December 9, 1965.

Wermuth, Thomas S., James M. Johnson and Christopher Pryslopski. *America's First River: The History and Culture of the Hudson River Valley*. Poughkeepsie, NY: Hudson River Valley Institute (Marist College) State University Press of New York, September 25, 2009, 164.

Bibliography

Werthheim, Stanley. *A Stephen Crane Encyclopedia*. Westport, CT: Greenwood Press, 1997, 56.

Wesselhoeft, Shew, Bedortha and Shieferdecker. "The Water Cure in America: Two Hundred and Twenty Cases of Various Diseases Treated with Water." In Horsell, William. *The Vegetarian Advocate*. Vol. 1. London: Wiley & Putnum, 1848–49.

West, Patricia. "Irish Immigrant Workers in Antebellum New York: The Experience of Domestic Servants at Van Buren's Lindenwald." *Hudson Valley Regional Review* 9, no. 2 (September 1992). http://www.nps.gov/mava/historyculture/upload/Lindenwald%20Servants.pdf.

Wetherbee, Martha, and Nathan Taylor. *Legend of the Bushwhacker Basket*. Sanbornton, NH: Martha Wetherbee Books, 1986, 8.

Wood, Jane. "It Can't Happen Here Again as Told by Frank Bailey." http://www.usgennet.org/usa/ny/county/columbia/stories/dr_bailey_part_1.htm.

"Yes Virginia, There Is a Santa Claus." http://en.wikipedia.org/wiki/Yes,_Virginia,_there_is_a_Santa_Claus (accessed January 2, 2014).

About the Author

Allison is a graduate of Fordham University in New York City with a degree in communications and creative writing. She spent much of her professional career in public relations in New York traveling throughout the world promoting health and fitness resorts. In her work as a writer, Allison has written plays and movie reviews, as well as short fiction, articles and essays on local people, places and history in her adopted home of Columbia County, New York.

She is a writer at heart and has history in her genes. Her family on her father's side has kept meticulous records of the Guertins, which date back to the early 1600s in Anjou, France.

Her love of history led her to her current position with the Edna St. Vincent Millay Society at Steepletop, located in Columbia County's town of Austerlitz. At the society, Allison is involved in raising funds to preserve the Pulitzer Prize–winning author's home and gardens while using her PR skills to illuminate the poet's large body of work.

About the Author

The idea of writing the *Hidden History of Columbia County* blossomed when she and her significant other, Adam, purchased a historic 1740s Colonial home in the village of Malden Bridge in the town of Chatham. She and Adam have lived there happily for over twenty years with their two cats and possibly several other previous inhabitants.